"As a mom, I think one of the [ ] for my children is pray for them. Praying remind [ ] God for their day-to-day and their future. Laine's book is an important reminder that God sees our needs, hears our hearts' cries and responds!"

Candace Cameron Bure, actress, producer
and *New York Times* bestselling author

"Laine's new book can help parents who are hurting find light and hope in the sometimes difficult yet always rewarding journey of raising a child."

Roma Downey, actress, producer and
New York Times bestselling author

"There is no doubt a battle going on for the hearts and minds of our young people today. Parents and those who work with kids are often shocked at the number of kids who are walking away from their faith and violating the values of their family. Yet there are very positive answers, and Laine Lawson Craft brings hope and healing in this book. It's a must-read! We can't let our guard down."

Jim Burns, PhD, president, HomeWord; author, *Doing Life with Your Adult Children* and *The Purity Code*

"*The Parent's Battle Plan* is an amazing and needed tool for parents in a day when our children, teens and young adults are facing overwhelming struggles, anxiety and depression. The stories of Laine's children and their own individual struggles and victories are relatable and encouraging. No more feeling alone in the challenges of parenting! This book will teach you how to pray and fight for your children."

Lisa Osteen Comes, author, *It's On the Way*
and *You Are Made for More!*

"Laine's book is full of applications and tools to restore hope and resurrect dreams the evil of this world may have stolen from your family and to bring your prodigal back home."

Alan and Lisa Robertson, *Duck Dynasty*

"Parenting in this dark world can often bring fear, confusion and desperation. We've seen and felt it in our own lives. Laine offers strategies in this must-read book that provide hope and healing to your family. One touch from God can change anything!"

Phil and Miss Kay Robertson, *Duck Dynasty*

"Parenting is not for wimps; we all need help. In her book, Lanie shares her personal experience with vulnerability and encourages the reader with practical applications for spiritual principles. You will be encouraged and equipped."

Ginger Stache, author, *Chasing Wonder*

THE
PARENT'S
BATTLE
PLAN

THE PARENT'S BATTLE PLAN

WARFARE STRATEGIES TO WIN
— BACK YOUR PRODIGAL —

LAINE LAWSON CRAFT

Chosen

a division of Baker Publishing Group
Minneapolis, Minnesota

Library of Congress Cataloging-in-Publication Data
Names: Craft, Laine Lawson, author.
Title: The parent's battle plan : warfare strategies to win back your prodigal / Laine Lawson Craft.
Description: Minneapolis, Minnesota : Chosen Books, a division of Baker Publishing Group, 2023.
Identifiers: LCCN 2022036447 | ISBN 9780800762841 (trade paper) | ISBN 9780800763145 (casebound) | ISBN 9781493439355 (ebook)
Subjects: LCSH: Spiritual warfare. | Parenting—Religious aspects—Christianity. | Child rearing—Religious aspects—Christianity.
Classification: LCC BV4509.5 .C733 2023 | DDC 235/.4—dc23/eng/20220909
LC record available at https://lccn.loc.gov/2022036447

23 24 25 26 27 28 29   7 6 5 4 3 2 1

First and foremost, I want to thank God for being my Father and partner through everything. My deepest, heartfelt thanks goes out to my amazing husband, Steve, who has fought for our family's unity and victory. To the bravest and most courageous three children I have ever known, I am so proud of how each of you fought the devil and *won*!

Contents

Introduction

Is your child slipping further and further away? There is nothing more important than the success of our family, particularly our children. We are in a war, but not with our teens and young adults. There is a darkness in the world that is enticing our children to step into paths of destruction. The good news is that there is a parent's battle plan with warfare strategies to win back our children.

There was a time in my life when all three of my teens and young adult children were in the pit of hell. Many of the decisions they made were robbing them of their future and any chance of having a successful life. They continually chose to travel down the dark roads of the enemy into which the world lured them. But God saved them!

If you are fighting similar battles with your teen or young adult and you feel as though you are losing, then you are in exactly the right place. If your child, adoptive child, grandchild or other young loved one is making self-destructive choices that have left his or her future in peril, you can still find the hope and the tools you need to fight hard and find victory. Every mission has a battle plan, and every war has a strategy.

In this book, I will share the prayers, Scripture passages, weapons, practical applications and tools that I have used and shared with other parents who are in the same battle. I want to provide the hope and guidance that causes us to be effective in the war for our children. We *can* take back what the enemy has stolen, but we must know the strategies that will activate our victory. Most importantly, we have to start today.

As you read through the following chapters, you will find revelations of the spiritual battles that face our families and children. You will uncover the secrets of the enemy and discover the weapons and tools that are already in your arsenal to win the battles. There are prayers, Scripture verses and practical applications that you can enact today. At the end of every chapter, you are given tactical strategies that you can implement immediately.

You do not have to wait one more second to be released from fear and defeat. You can begin utilizing the weapons and strategies for war now. You can recognize the darkness and bring light to the circumstances that will enable you to fight without fear. You will be empowered to face whatever is tossed your way, enabling you to defend your family all the way to victory!

Do not let your children slip any further away. They cannot do it on their own. They need our help. Let's win the battle together. Do not let another day pass. Begin your battle for and with them today.

PART ONE

GETTING READY
FOR BATTLE

Parental Expectations

There are an estimated 385,000 babies born in the world each and every day. Most of us remember the very first moment we were informed that a special delivery was headed our way. Maybe it involved a pregnancy test that turned positive, or maybe it included a phone call that confirmed the exciting news. Some of us planned for a long time and awaited the exciting day when we could bring our newly adopted baby home. The nursery and all the frills were already installed for the newest addition to our family, and we pined for the day when we would hear the word *finalized*.

Perhaps we were the proud grandparents who were awaiting a tiny human to finally spoil and love on relentlessly. Aunts, uncles and all the rest of our loved ones shared in the nail-biting process. Whether we were fostering, adopting or giving birth, whether we were parents, grandparents or close friends, we all knew one thing for sure—we were going to celebrate this new baby. And it was in that moment that the dreams and hopes concerning our children began to flood *our* hearts.

In various and perhaps random order, we start experimenting with names, listening to how the phonetics roll off our tongues. We discuss legacy names such as Charles the III or Penelope who would be named after Grandmother Penny. We may even go as far as to investigate what specific names mean or who they remind us of in historical terms. We consider favorite figures who have achieved great things and ponder whether the name represents a part of their legacy.

We may also choose *not* to use a specific name because its base definition or translation is negative. I have a friend who has the name Melanie, which is translated commonly as *melancholy*. Hmm. That seems like something one would definitely want to take into consideration. In her case, her mother was obsessed with a character from Margaret Mitchell's novel, *Gone with the Wind*. She explained to me that the character was above and beyond in the integrity column, and for her, that superseded any definition. On a side note, she is a very upbeat individual.

Finally, we may be the type of parent who is determined to give our child a name that stands out from those listed in the published name books. That is when we find ourselves doodling various spellings and googling the most popular names in the world to avoid those choices. When imagination takes over, we often see the results as well. Orlando Bloom and Katy Perry have a child named Daisy Dove. Jay Z and Beyonce endowed their child with Blue Ivy. Ryan Gosling and Eva Mendes have Esmeralda Amada. In essence, anything goes when it comes to picking out how you will refer to your prized newborn.

Then it is time to focus on the purchases necessary to sustain new life. We debate over cribs, cradles and car seats in an effort to create a fun, safe and unique place for our children to call home. That includes an overall education for each piece purchased. We learn, for example, that there can be no more than two-and-three-eighths inches (about the width of a soda can) between crib slats so that a baby's head cannot fit through them. There are to be no corner posts over one-sixteenth of an inch so clothing cannot catch. Everything has parameters that contribute to some facet of our children's lives.

As we build the environment that will eventually house our young family members, our minds are fast at work fashioning a hopeful future. When the moment of arrival occurs, our amazement only increases. We see how pure, innocent and vulnerable our children are and how much they need protection.

As we revel in the joy, giggles and unbridled laughter that bubbles out of their tiny body, our commitment only grows stronger—as does our dream for his or her future. Is she the future president of a big corporation? Of our nation? He seems to love the doctor play set more than his other toys. Is that a sign of his future? Will he invent tools that cure disease or save the world? Will she heed a calling from God and bring forth the greatest revival of all time? Our parental aspirations in the early stages of their lives are limitless.

Somewhere between the dreams and the reality of raising our children, there exists another force to be reckoned with. In fact, there is often a major battle being waged over our children and, consequently, against our entire family. In the midst of everything else that goes on from day to day, we often cannot foresee the traps that have been set. We are often so focused on what is the best that when the worst arrives it is absolutely unexpected.

We never envision our children chasing after the next "fix," whether it is drugs, alcohol, porn or some other gateway to destruction. We fail to imagine our children being arrested or fighting a depression that is so deeply engrained that suicidal thoughts are a daily occurrence. We simply do not see any of it coming. Perhaps you have a child, like mine, who had begun living in the way you had hoped, but who has now made bad choices.

Our story begins with me sitting in my recliner on Mother's Day sobbing hysterically. My dreams and aspirations for all my children lay in tattered pieces. Truly awful thoughts were circling over and over in my mind. *Are my children going to survive? Will they live to be 25 years old? Will my sons end up dead, addicted or in prison? Will my daughter find true happiness and worth?* My heart was shattered into a million pieces. I did not know how I could go on, but I knew that I somehow had to keep moving.

I know from experience that there is nothing worse than watching our children fall backward unexpectedly from the path we prayed for daily. The disappointment can be paralyzing. The children we once knew seem to have all but disappeared. Gone are the joy, laughter, trust and hopeful future we spent so much time daydreaming about. In their place are a fear and dread of what might be coming next.

Our responsibility, as parents, includes certain vows much like those of marriage. So many of us recited the "for better or worse" clause when we committed ourselves to our spouses. With our children, we agreed in essence to the same and more. What we may not have understood at the time was the fact that there were others who would do their best to take them away from us.

In a marriage if things get really, really bad, it is possible to separate without divorcing. It is also possible to agree to table discussions on specific topics until both parties are ready to address them. The same cannot be said for our relationships with our children. Most of the time, we are ensconced inside the house with them through thick and thin. A teen will seldom agree to table anything. They tend to communicate in emotional outbursts.

So beyond putting a roof over their heads and food in their mouths for an extended period, we also have the joy—and sometimes the misery—of sitting on the front row in their theater of life. Due to age considerations, we also have the job of doing our best to clean up the messes to their reputations and status that they leave behind in the world. Marriage is not the same as child rearing. Parenting has its own set of complex conditions.

Our Children Belonged to God First

No matter what we are facing with our children, there is one—and only one—fact to which we can cling during the lowest times of chaos. *Our children belonged to God before they were lent to us.* When we were busy dreaming about what color hair our child would have or what gender our loved one was going to be, God already knew. There is a huge difference between what we did and what He did to usher them into the world. God literally called them into existence.

God is all-seeing and all-knowing. Nothing exists outside of Him, and nothing happens without His knowledge. The Bible tells us, "Before I formed you in the womb I knew you, before you were born I set you apart; I appointed you as a prophet to the nations" (Jeremiah 1:5). This demonstrates His foreknowledge of children. When God speaks to Jeremiah, He prefers him to know of his origin. This means every human, including our child, has a relationship with his or her Creator from pre-birth to the afterlife. It is truly an eternal partnership.

If God brought our children into existence, then it follows suit that He specifically entrusted them to us. He intends us to love and care for them throughout their lives. The Bible includes many tips and guidelines on how to do that. Most of us have heard the declaration, "Train up a child in the way he should go, even when he grows older he will not abandon it" (Proverbs 22:6 NASB). There is no doubt that, as parents, we all try to do that very thing. Some of our children, however, have to run interference with an unseen enemy that can alter their paths greatly. Depending on how much they listen to our advice versus how much they listen to outside influences, this verse may seem beyond impossible to stand on or believe.

And that is just what dark influences would have us do. It is our job not to go down the proverbial rabbit hole with our children. We are, instead, to choose to fight to bring them back into our plane of existence. Although we may be tempted to give up or feel we have failed, God still believes in our ability to walk through "better or worse" with them. He will give us the strength to get through it all.

Two Sets of Eyes and Ears

As believers, we have two types of eyes and ears—one pair of each that is visible on our bodies and the others that are invisible. They both have a distinction and purpose. Our visible organs need very little explanation. If you glance in the mirror, they display themselves prominently. Eyes and ears have the job of reporting sensory information. They help us perform practical functions, provide us with sensory delight and serve as a radar for surrounding danger. A child riding his or her bike in the street has ears that warn him or her when an oncoming car emits a honk. The movie industry thrives on eyes and ears. We flock to the theater to check out the latest superheroes, romantic comedies and historical drama films.

Our second set of eyes and ears is a spiritual mechanism that operates in correlation with the Holy Spirit. They, too, gather data, but a different type. Spiritual instruction comes in alignment with God's promises and the eternal truth of His Word. This information often demands that we look beyond what our natural eyes and ears are digesting to comprehend a hope, vision and future that God is working to bring about.

There are other differences between the natural and spiritual. Our physical eyes and ears can be less than perfect for a variety of reasons. Some are born with 20/20 eyesight, but as they age, that changes. Others may have less than perfect sight from the start. The same is true for hearing. And there are those who must navigate life completely without sight, sound or both. Human invention has made great strides in both fields as far as creating products that compensate, such as hearing aids, contact lenses and glasses, but there is still room to grow.

Spiritual eyes and ears, however, work in another way. While some may be endowed with great spiritual acumen from the start, there is no reason why the rest of us cannot catch up. The closer our relationship with God and the more time we invest in seeking Him, the greater our spiritual capacity. In times of distress, it is imperative that we strive to obtain the best spiritual sight and hearing possible. God is our only source for looking past the ugly that might be occurring in our child's life to the place where victory resides.

God's Purpose for Our Children

God has always had a purpose for our children's lives, just as we have. "'For I know the plans I have for you,' declares the LORD, 'plans to prosper you and not to harm you, plans to give you hope and a future'" (Jeremiah 29:11). This is what He intends for all His people. The dreams we have for our children have not been in vain. His promises are still in force, and they are not going anywhere.

As time goes on and we get to know our children better, many of us start to fabricate more concrete plans for them. Interestingly, we often fail to realize that we have not included God in the process. As I watched my two sons and daughter grow, I could see great things in them.

Steven was so smart. He had a photographic memory. I was amazed that he could stand at the end of his bed, take an initial look over pages and pages of information for a test, peruse them one more time and then remember the content of every page. It was obvious to me early on that Steven would master academics and had the intellect to excel at anything his heart desired.

Lawson was totally different from Steven. He was incredible with his hands. From an early age, he would pull things apart and then meticulously put the many pieces back together. His inner drive for success and accomplishment was amazingly evident. He never entertained failure. Very early on, we started thinking of him as a successful future entrepreneur.

Kaylee, our only daughter, had artistic flair and was so gifted. In a relatively small amount of time, she would create beautiful sketches. Kaylee had a unique eye and would pair unpredictable colors together perfectly. She was creative with many mediums of art. Everything she envisioned and placed on canvas became a piece of art that everyone wanted to display. We were convinced that one day her art would be the passion and the means of Kaylee's success.

Perhaps you could see similar aspects of significance in your own children. Your John built unique and towering structures out of his Legos. Or your Aggie was fretting continually about her outfits and always insisted on adding an additional flair before considering herself dressed for the third grade. It is not hard to nurse the idea of a future architect or fashion designer, because all of our aspirations are fueled by the immense love within our hearts.

Yet as the battle for our children rages, it often becomes apparent that God's plans for them may not be the same as we have outlined succinctly in our heads. He may, in fact, have a completely different path in mind for them. That is when we must make the distinction of who Thomas or Megan belonged to before we were entrusted with his or her care.

As we watch our mental sandcastles crumble beneath the weight of the erroneous paths and decisions of our children, we come to a crossroad, a moment of truth. Are we going to stand on the promises of God, or are we going to accept that all is lost?

Our children may not be exhibiting the potential today that we originally saw and that caused us to believe they were to fulfill their purposes, but God sees all that they are *still* capable of doing—even if we cannot envision what that might look like. As parents, God still intends us to be viable in enabling His purposes for them. We can and should continue to stand in the gap and intercede on their behalf. We are to remain in partnership with Him for the future of our children.

It is time to ask ourselves if our plan or God's plan is the one that matters—and if we know the difference. In the end, does it really matter if our notions of their successful futures do not match their early beginnings? Are we able to be more than pleased with any end product that is supplied by God that leaves them whole and healthy?

A LESSON IN PERSPECTIVE

What parents never expect

- ► a teenager who drinks too much
- ► a girl who is defiant and rebellious
- ► a boy who is angry all the time
- ► a young adult struggling with purpose
- ► a teenager with low self-esteem

What God still sees

- ► His own masterpiece (see Ephesians 2:10)
- ► a work in progress (see Philippians 1:6)
- ► each able to heal from anything (see Jeremiah 33:6)
- ► divine assignments for each (see Ephesians 1:4)
- ► accepted and loved (see 1 John 3:1–2)

WHAT CAN I DO TODAY?

Make the decision to pray for your child every single day. Start by writing the following on an index card and reciting it at every opportunity:

> "For I know the plans I have for you," declares the LORD, "plans to prosper you and not to harm you, plans to give you hope and a future."
>
> Jeremiah 29:11

Dear Lord,
You have good plans for _____ (your child's name).

🕊 PRAYER OF THANKSGIVING

Father, I thank You that I can come to You today on behalf of my child. I know that You love my family even more than I do. I also know You hear my most profound concerns. Help me to trust You with all that stands in the way of my family serving You. Help me to adjust any attitudes that do not align with Your will for my child. Thank You for helping to heal my broken heart. I rest my hope in You as I battle for my child. Help me to use my spiritual eyes and ears to hear Your voice and follow Your instructions on this journey. In Jesus' name, Amen.

The Invisible Battle

When our cell phone battery is kaput, we search quickly to find a power source to charge it up. Even though we cannot actually see the electricity flowing into the cord and charging the battery, we end up with a fully powered phone.

So it goes with the spiritual realm. Just because we cannot physically see what is going on spiritually does not mean that the spiritual world does not exist or that it does not hold the ultimate power. Still, *unlike* the process for charging our phones, it is vital that we take a look at the power sources of both sides in play. Remember that we are in a war. It is not a war against other people or countries; instead, it is a spiritual war that is taking place beyond our natural eyes.

As believers, we face an enemy named Satan. He is a deadly force that attacks our weaknesses, emotions, thoughts and doubts. He even goes as far as attempting to induce us to question our beliefs. Though we cannot see our attacker, this warfare is very real, and it manifests itself in physical behavior. The interplay between spiritual evil and human beings is common. These same battles are waged in the lives and minds of our children. He can wrap himself around their thought processes and their self-image and, most of all, cause self-destructive choices to the point where their lives are in danger.

Our Common Behaviors

When our babies are small, we are often told their sudden bursts of bad behavior can be attributed to an underlying need for attention. There is a fairly good possibility the experts who say this are completely correct. Growing up is not easy, and we should expect common behavior problems that have nothing to do with anything other than a stretch on the maturity scale that we all navigate.

There are several common behaviors we have all struggled to master. They fall under four basic categories: self-control, obedience, expressing ourselves verbally and the treatment of others. It is likely that we have all gone through life lessons with our children around these topics. Little Tommy had to learn that it was not okay to stop and urinate in the backyard while he was playing. It took Sally a while to understand that no matter how much she cried and moaned, she was only going to get one cookie from the jar. Harry figured out eventually that when he asked to go to the park, his parents accommodated most of the time. And Beverly endured a trip to the principal's office and a bit of punishment before she realized she should tell her fellow student to move off her mat rather than lean over to bite her. These all represent simple trials of comprehending how the world works.

Then comes the day when sixteen-year-old Nicole's grades suddenly start slipping, and she no longer wants to go to school. It is so disconcerting that Mom takes her to the doctor to rule out anything physical before trying counseling. Mom eventually has no choice but to discipline her for skipping school. Still, nothing is working. She may very well have stepped into the place in which it is time to consider who she is really fighting.

It is because our enemy is so cruel and deceptive that we must know how to defend ourselves and our children, in coordination with God, to obtain victory in this battle for our families. It is the ultimate battle of good versus evil, and it all takes place in the spiritual realm.

Many of us have never been made aware of the truth of spiritual warfare. We need to become educated and be instructed on the necessities and truths associated with this warfare so that we know how to use knowledge to our advantage. The enemy would prefer us to be ignorant of his tactics, lies, deceptions and all his other schemes. If we never talk about it or acknowledge that there is a battle going on over our lives, then the enemy is better equipped to attack us and create hell on earth.

The prophet Elisha was on a mission for the Lord, but the king of Aram wanted to kill Elisha (see 2 Kings 6). We read that Elisha was being chased down by a powerful troop of soldiers, horses and chariots. At night they entered the city where Elisha was sleeping. When Elisha's servant woke him the next morning, he was surrounded by an army. The servant ran to Elisha with fear and asked, "What should we do?"

Elisha prayed to God, "Open his eyes, LORD, so that he may see" (verse 17). The Lord opened the servant's eyes. When he looked out, he saw that the hills were full of horses and chariots of fire specifically sent by God to defend Elisha. Amazing! What no one else could see in the natural, God allowed the servant to see. There were spiritual soldiers warring on behalf of Elisha.

God is the same yesterday, today and tomorrow (see Hebrews 13:8). He is a God that does not change. If God was able to show the servant the soldiers of spiritual warfare, then He certainly can do the same today. We are in battle with an enemy that we may not be able to see, but God is with us fighting on our behalf in the spiritual realm.

It is not hard to see things from the standpoint of what we physically witness in a day. It takes no effort whatsoever to look at the clock and know with absolute certainty that it is time to get up and go to work. We can also work through particular aspects of our environment with the assistance of human wisdom (the culmination of all that we have learned so far). If the temperature drops to freezing, our previous experience tells us to grab our coat, hat and gloves before going out the door.

But stretching our minds to accept that there is a spiritual realm in play can be quite a challenge. This comes as no surprise to God. He made sure to make it plain in His Word so that there could be no argument.

An Unseen World

The Bible speaks of an unseen world that is parallel to ours. One of the most exciting and revelatory passages occurs in 1 Corinthians. The apostle Paul explains that the only reason he is able to share the Gospel is because he received the information from the spiritual realm. "This is what we speak, not in words taught us by human wisdom but in words taught by the Spirit, explaining spiritual realities with Spirit-taught words" (1 Corinthians 2:13). We are all capable of receiving insight and instruction from God. The question is whether or not we can accept and act on that fact.

Some of us may have faith roots, but we have never really engaged in an intimate relationship with God. Others may have been so defeated that we feel as though God has forgotten us. And possibly you have never been exposed to this God of the Bible, the Creator of all. As I look back to earlier years of my life, I think I always knew there was more to God than I was experiencing.

My faith was born inside of a religion where musical instruments were not used. The music was all *a cappella*, and honestly, for me, very dull. There certainly were not any prayer languages (or tongues) ever spoken. As a matter of fact, such gifts were considered dead gifts. They believed that after the time that Jesus died and ascended, these gifts were never again used. Many churches refrain from using the word *miracles*. Why is that? Do they believe that God no longer performs miracles? Gifts of prophecy are shunned by many. Is prophesy considered dead? Has that gift been withheld? Basically, too many believe that once Jesus ascended into heaven, miracles, signs and wonders were dead.

I was not aware of the true spiritual realm until my life was falling apart and my heart was shattered into a million pieces. My marriage was dead. Our financial status was near bankruptcy. Kaylee was very sick, and the boys were tweens experiencing real-life challenges. Religion was not working.

Remember the fairy-tale story of how Humpty Dumpty sat on a wall and had a great fall and no one could put him back together again? That was me. My world, my life and everything in it were beyond repair. The mindset of living right, doing right and going to church was not accomplishing a thing. Finally, in the deepest and darkest pit of my life, I dared God.

I yelled out to Him, "God if You are really real and moving supernaturally today, then please rescue me!" I was crying hysterically. Truthfully, I had nowhere else to go and no one else to turn to in the world. My only hope was that God would answer. And He did answer. I was touched profoundly and immediately with a sense of warmth that I had never felt before. It literally burned inside my chest and all throughout my entire body. This was the turning point of my life. This is where I began to understand and see that there was definitely a spiritual world. I could not see it, but there was no doubt that it existed.

There is a real God who moves on our behalf and has ways to work behind the scenes and touch us even in our darkest hour or in the midst of our shameful sins. God is the power that created the universe. He is one being in three Persons, in the power of God, the Holy Spirit through the agency of God and the Son, Jesus Christ. This is the Trinity of God. He created us to be His own children. He loves us extravagantly and wants to bless us and exist with us in an intimate, Father-child relationship.

Faith Is Vital

A lot of religious preference is given to our personality styles. I am gregarious and outgoing, and I love excitement. Those who have tamer tendencies would have been very comfortable in the environment I experienced. Either way, we all strive to make church life comfortable.

But there are other things to consider. If we ensconce ourselves in churches that do not promote the awe-inspiring power of God and His willingness to partner with those He created to do battle with our enemies, we are missing the most vital component of our Christian faith. The most important part of our faith is to recognize that we move and act through the power of God. This does not have to revolve around four church walls.

Every mission has a battle plan, so if our personal mission is to win the spiritual war, then we must have faith. Faith gives us the courage to battle. Faith is the hope that God will give us victory even when we cannot see how it will be won. Faith is the anchor that keeps us tied to God inside the raging storms. All of this is found in our personal search for God and in His presence. We are His children and His Church. Faith is found when we seek God with all our hearts.

We can also begin to connect with others to build our faith and do life together. This faith is the key to knowing that God will equip and empower us—no matter how big the battle we are facing. The Bible gives us the definition of faith. "Now faith is the substance of things hoped for, the evidence of things not seen" (Hebrews 11:1 NKJV).

We know that there are others who came before us who exhibited this type of belief. The list is huge, but here are three superstars. Noah believed an unseen warning and ignored the fear of man's ridicule as he built the ark that saved his family. Abraham believed in an unseen land and a promise from God that he would be the father of nations. He set out on his journey and left everything that he called home at the age of seventy-five. Sarah believed in an unseen conception despite her age, and she gave birth to Isaac when she was ninety. We should strive to develop the level of faith that has been demonstrated in their stories.

Conversely, and simply put from the living Word of God, Satan is the devil who opposes God. He can be called the "evil one." The first reference to Satan can be found in Genesis. He is described as "more crafty than any other beast of the field that the LORD God had made" (3:1 ESV). God created Satan, too. Unfortunately, he turned against God, which makes him our enemy. Satan is described as an angel who rejected God's authority and tried to persuade others to follow his rebellious ways (see Revelation 12:7–9; Jude 6; 2 Peter 2:4). God threw this defiant angel down to earth with his followers—where the war against good and evil began.

The good news is that, as hard as he might try to turn the tide by interfering with our lives, Satan has already been defeated. Jesus Christ died on a cross and gave all of us eternal victory over Satan. The devil has never been a match for our Savior, Jesus Christ, and he never will be. Satan has no power over us on an eternal scale; however, that does not stop him from engaging in a battle over our lives through spiritual warfare.

Scripture gives us many descriptions of who the devil is and how he fights over us. Jesus called him the father of lies. He is a deceiver. He is cunning. He masquerades as an angel of light. He is out to seek, kill and destroy us. He roams around like a lion seeking to devour all of us. We must know our enemy well so that we can battle against him more effectively for eternal victory. He and his dark army stay busy setting traps for all of us, especially for the most vulnerable: our children. The best way to avoid him and to protect our family is to know his tactics and stand up against him.

Primarily, Satan wants you to doubt God's Word and His existence. Remember that God is the perfect Father. Yet His own children, Adam and Eve, sinned against Him because they doubted Him. The enemy, in the form of a snake, slightly altered God's words, twisting them just enough for Eve to doubt why God would instruct them not eat the fruit of the Tree of Life (see Genesis 3:1–5).

The devil made it appear that the reason was because God was withholding something from them or saying no to them. Enticements and temptations from the devil eventually made Eve question God, which led her to disobey God. We, too, can fall under these temptations from Satan. If he can make you question your faith, question who God really is or convince you that God's Word is not relevant today, then he has you under his demonic influence.

He wants us to live in fear. The essence of our battle becomes faith over fear. It is interesting that the Bible includes well over 365 verses on fear and anxiety. That means there is at least one for every day of the year. God also gave the direct command to "fear not" in over one hundred instances. Obviously, God has a lot to say about the subject of fear.

Additionally, the devil wants to separate us from God through sin and shame. He knows if he can get you to succumb to lust, pride or rebellion, then you will live in condemnation and run from God. Almost all of these self-serving behaviors contain the facet of keeping secrets. We would never admit we lust for another's spouse. We do not think of commonly announcing that we consider ourselves better in some area than those around us. Interestingly, what we might think we are to keep to ourselves is the very thing that is able to lead us to taking up residence with Satan.

The irony in this is that we are not fooling anyone—especially God. "Whenever our heart condemns us, God is greater than our heart, and he knows everything" (1 John 3:20 ESV). Once we are aware of how these deceptions affect us and our entire family, then we can maneuver our way around them so that we do not get stuck indefinitely.

As parents, we can unveil how the ruler of darkness operates. We can refuse to let ignorance about the truth of God's light and power (which is the enemy's greatest weapon against us) prevail and take down our children. The more we know about God and the more we gain insight into the character, strategies and operational tactics of Satan's army, the better we are equipped to overcome. Knowing who God is and who our archenemy is will establish our roles as spiritual warriors for our children. We can expose Satan for who he is and interrupt his evil intent.

Even more satisfying is the confidence we gain after we begin to understand that we have been given every weapon we need for this war and victory is ours. We are meant to walk boldly—not in arrogance, but humility—and stand up for what we believe. Boldness can be translated in many ways.

It can begin with making the decision to step out of our comfort zone to do whatever is necessary for the sake of our children. It also means that we operate as Hebrews instructs and "come boldly to the throne of grace, that we may obtain mercy and find grace to help in time of need" (4:16 NKJV). It takes great spiritual revelation to continue to fight numerous and intense battles. We have to know and believe throughout our very core that we are not at war with our prodigal children—we are at war with the devil.

The moment I realized that demons were as real as the heavenly angels and that these demons truly had taken on the mission to kill, steal and destroy my children, I froze. Shock and massive fear coursed through me. But shortly afterward came the realization that Jesus came to give us everything we need to win the war. When we truly believe that God is the same yesterday, today and tomorrow, meaning He is a God who does not change, then our faith takes on a massive potential to grow. God really can do the impossible! We are correct in believing He will supply power, protection, peace and perseverance. And all it takes is our comprehension and belief.

 **BE AWARE**

Do not fall for it

▶ the devil is not real

▶ I have no power over Satan

▶ I cannot outlast his attacks against me or my children

▶ I should fear him

The truth is

▶ "For our struggle is not against flesh and blood, but against the rulers, against the powers, against the world forces of this darkness, against the spiritual forces of wickedness in the heavenly places" (Ephesians 6:12 NASB).

▶ "I have given you the power to trample on snakes and scorpions and to defeat the power of your enemy Satan. Nothing can harm you" (Luke 10:19 CEV).

▶ "Therefore do not cast away your confidence, which has great reward. For you have need of endurance, so that after you have done the will of God, you may receive the promise" (Hebrews 10:35–36 NKJV).

▶ "For God has not given us a spirit of fear and timidity, but of power, love, and self-discipline" (2 Timothy 1:7 NLT).

 **WHAT CAN I DO TODAY?**

Acknowledge that you are in a spiritual war. Start by writing the following on an index card and reciting it at every opportunity:

> For the weapons of our warfare are not of the flesh but have divine power to destroy strongholds.
>
> 2 Corinthians 10:4 ESV

Dear Lord,
I am partnering with You to fight this battle for
_____ *(your child's name).*

PRAYER FOR THE BATTLE

Father, thank You for lifting the veil off my spiritual eyes to show me that Satan is real. I have complete faith that You will deliver my child from the traps that the enemy has set. Please reveal more of who You are as I seek Your presence and Your instructions about how to handle my family's circumstances. I believe that You will expose the evil in our midst and provide every weapon needed to overcome it. In Jesus' name, Amen.

A Look at the Dark Army

God's army is partially comprised of angels. Of the four types of angels in the Bible, the cherubim are mentioned the most. Ezekiel provides us with a rather daunting description. "For each had four faces and four wings and what looked like human hands under their wings" (Ezekiel 10:21 NLT). It was this type of angel that was placed on the east side of the Garden of Eden to guard the Tree of Life.

The seraphim are mentioned the least. They are only found in the book of Isaiah and are seen flying above the Lord as He sits on the throne. "Above him were seraphim, each with six wings: With two wings they covered their faces, with two they covered their feet, and with two they were flying" (Isaiah 6:2).

The third type of angel is the archangel, from the Greek word *archangelos*, which is translated as "chief angel."[1] The only archangel directly referred to by name in the Bible is

Michael. Most people consider Michael a warrior angel due to his participation in a battle found in Revelation. "And war broke out in heaven: Michael and his angels fought with the dragon; and the dragon and his angels fought" (12:7 NKJV). While the Bible does not say so directly, Gabriel (mentioned in the first chapter of the book of Luke and in chapter nine of the book of Daniel) is also considered an archangel by most Christians. And that brings us to the fourth type: fallen angels.

The Bible explains how the beginning of evil on earth started with an archangel named Lucifer (see Ezekiel 28). He held the highest rank within the angels and was considered to be one of God's favorites. Can you imagine? He had access to God and walked in communion with Him day and night. What more could you want? Unfortunately, Lucifer's pride and ego consumed him.

Soon after that, he *did* want more. In fact, he conceived a plan to achieve his own desires. Lucifer, later to be known as Satan, conspired with other angels to overthrow the Creator. We can see the plan in Isaiah when God let Lucifer know that He knew what was going on.

> "But you said in your heart, 'I will ascend to heaven; I will raise my throne above the stars of God, and I will sit on the mount of assembly in the recesses of the north. I will ascend above the heights of the clouds; I will make myself like the Most High.'"
>
> Isaiah 14:13–14 NASB

Satan saw no need for his Lord and envisioned himself seated on God's throne. What followed was inevitable. Due to Lucifer's rebellion, God was forced to cast him and all of the other angels who participated in the uprising out of heaven and down to earth. Lucifer and company were effectively and completely separated from God. They also were classified from that point on, particularly in God's eyes, as Satan and his demons.

The Dark Army Knows Our Children

What does this have to do with our children? These spiritual beings are roaming the earth today searching for human hosts within which they can operate. Evil circumstances, influences and consequences are executed through these demons.

The demons have the ability to blind our children so that they can no longer see the path of light (see 2 Corinthians 4:4). They can oppress and deceive our children in ways that would be hard for us to imagine, and they can do this so that it presents differently from child to child (see Matthew 24:3–5). This spiritual interference with our children often shows up initially as a relatively innocuous behavior that is not natural to the child we know (see 2 Corinthians 11:14). We often do not recognize that something crucial has changed both in and around them.

I will never forget my utter surprise and dismay when rebellion showed up in each of my children. It seemed to come from nowhere. At first, just as with Lucifer, there seemed to be a touch of arrogance and pride that I attributed to a growing independence. At the time, they saw little reason to heed me as any type of authority around particular topics. Little by little I found myself working harder than usual to get through our normal routines. As time progressed, they graduated to outright defiant behavior and rebellion.

Until his sixteenth year of life, my son Lawson was the kindest, sweetest child. He was soft spoken and shy. I knew he was a very special child because he was gifted with so many unique and wonderful qualities. He was amazing at working with his hands, and he constructed and designed various projects. To this day, he can take apart almost any motor and put it back together. It seemed as if Lawson was enjoying the all-American, faith-filled and blessed teenaged life. But looking back, I know that in one moment Lawson's life shifted from being a light to being a boy who was cast into the darkness of hell.

It was Lawson's ninth-grade year. On one ordinary night in January, he decided to go to a store to buy a pack of cigarettes. I learned later that it was a common stop for sixteen-year-olds. Like so many teenagers, he had a fake ID. Mind you, Lawson was about five feet four and weighed maybe 120 pounds. He was small in stature and kept to himself. There is no way that he looked legal. He stepped into the store, asked to buy the cigarettes and handed over the fake ID. He was successful in the purchase. But the next thing he knew, Lawson was handcuffed and thrown into the back of a police car. There he sat, shocked, scared and shaking.

It was my daughter Kaylee's ninth-grade year when she decided to ask a few friends over while my husband and I were out of town. We lived in a small town, and it often happened that when kids would have a party while their parents were gone, kids from all other areas would show up uninvited. We had shared with our kids that we were aware of what was going on in other homes. I remember emphasizing the dangers. "Don't have parties while we are gone because they can quickly get out of hand if people that you don't know show up."

A few friends who Kaylee had invited to attend started to arrive at the party. Then a few more friends showed up. All was peaceful. But eventually, a large number of other teenagers drove up from other towns and neighborhoods. After that, the party scene quickly got out of control. Kaylee had to call her older nephew for support. He came over to our home to run all of the guests—both known and unknown—out of the house. Kaylee was left with a disaster.

When we found out we were so upset. We had never dreamed Kaylee would do anything of this sort. Our house had been ransacked and scoured through by people we had never met. The most painful part of the entire experience was that she knew not to have friends over when we were not at home. Our trust was broken. We were shocked that our sweet Kaylee was even capable of something like this.

Our Steven was entering the seventh grade. He was our firstborn and the first to go to junior high. A few weeks after school started, a friend invited him to his first high school football game. The plan was that the friend and his father would pick Steven up, go to dinner and then go to the game. We were so excited. Steven was quiet and shy, and this was to be his first real social event without us around. The friend and his dad came to the house and picked Steven up. They proceeded to go to a restaurant, a honky-tonk, and eat dinner. Why the dad stayed inside while Steven and his two friends wandered out into the parking lot I will never know.

It was then that things took a definite turn for the worse. Steven's friends pulled out a knife and began slashing the tires of the restaurant patrons. I do not think Steven had ever touched a tire, but even if he had, who could have prepared him for this madness? His friend did this damage without anyone being aware. Eventually, they all continued to the game without a word being spoken.

The people whose tires were slashed left the restaurant to discover a myriad of flat tires. Thank God no one got hurt; nonetheless, these patrons immediately reported the incident to the restaurant, and they began to look into who could have done such a thing. The following Monday at school there was a campus-wide announcement. Students were asked to tell the principal if they knew anything.

Steven turned himself in and explained the details to the principal. This was honorable, but Steven received punishment for what the other kids had done. All three of the boys became outcasts. Steven gained the ugly nickname "Slasher." This horrible moniker followed him and his siblings all the way through their schooling. The experience was the beginning of a traumatic journey that lasted way past his high school years.

We were devastated. We knew, in retrospect, that Steven had no idea how to handle this awful situation, but he did the right thing. You can imagine how devastating it was that he never lived it down. For a long time we did not realize that Steven had begun a downward spiral that lasted for many, many years.

Separating Behavior

Perhaps my stories resonate with you as a parent. If so, then it is time to separate the behavior from the child. The angels of darkness (also known as demons) are our true enemy, not our children. It is hard to keep this in the forefront of our minds as our children's eyes turn cold and we feel as though they are disconnected from the love we continually offer, but it is imperative that we do. It is true that they are not totally blameless in their actions, but they are also being guided by powers of which they are probably not aware.

As children, most of us knew no more about the devil than the Halloween costume we saw. He was just the guy dressed in red with horns, a pitchfork and maybe a long, pointed tail. Think back to what you knew when you were the age your child is right now. You probably were not a wealth of knowledge on the mechanics of spiritual warfare—and neither are they. The goal is that you see the whole picture when you look at your child and not only outward symptoms.

When we see unusual behavior in a child we know very well, it is time to consider whether or not they are under demonic attack. And it helps to know the goals of the enemy. The primary battle plan, on the evil side, is to distract us from standing in prayer, agreeing with God and, consequently, handing over the future of our children. If we get so angry at their behavior that we sit and stew for days or are so brokenhearted that we cry for hours and then fall into an extended depression, our actions can give the dark army the time it needs to cause even further damage. Inactivity in the spiritual realm on one side means the other side is gaining ground. We cannot afford to be blinded to what is really going on and who is orchestrating the thoughts that are leading to our children's behavior.

Let's face a few facts. Demons have immortality until the end times when Jesus comes back for the second and last time. That means they have an invulnerability that makes them impervious to any damage or injury that does not come straight from God. Ultimately, they will be condemned to hell for eternity. In fact, Jesus came to the earth as a mere man for the very purpose of destroying the devil's work.

While Satan is considered the "prince of demons," the others thrown down from heaven to earth consisted of varying types, just as in God's army (see Ephesians 2:2; 6:12). Their only purpose is to roam the earth looking for any weaknesses in humans that will enable them to take control. They gather information on our habits, actions and personality traits that allows them to develop successful strategies of action. Throughout the Bible, we are shown how Satan and the dark army can take possession of people and render them helpless. "Then one was brought to Him who was demon-possessed, blind and mute; and He healed him, so that the blind and mute man both spoke and saw" (Matthew 12:22 NKJV).

We cannot afford to let the word *possession* intimidate us. It simply means that we are more susceptible to being lured toward temptations that are introduced and guided by an evil spirit. First and foremost, believers are children of the Most High, which means that all of us are fully able to throw off any spirits in the name of Jesus!

Most importantly, demons can gang up on the most precious gifts God has bestowed upon us—our vulnerable children whose faith is still in its baby form. This fact makes them particularly open to dark army suggestions. Luke explains the process that takes place when our children's behavior goes from bad to worse.

> "When an impure spirit comes out of person, it goes through arid places seeking rest and does not find it. Then it says, 'I will return to the house I left.' When it arrives, it finds the house swept clean and put in order. Then it goes and takes seven other spirits more wicked than itself, and they go in and live there. And the final condition of that person is worse than the first."
>
> Luke 11:24–26

We Can Defeat Them!

No matter how difficult things seem, the child we know and love is still alive on the inside. It is our responsibility, in partnership with God, to step up and fight hard to defeat the dark army so that demons are forced to flee. We are then to keep praying to keep our children safe from additional harm.

As in any critical circumstance, the more information we gather, the better. This is no exception. This is a battle we can win, but we must stand firm and learn to fight. The Bible lets us know that it is a battle we are well able to wage. "And they cast out many demons and healed many sick people, anointing them with olive oil" (Mark 6:13 NLT). What God has allowed one to do, He intends for all of us to do. As strange as it might seem to some of us, we are capable of doing anything any other human has done. The key is to believe it.

The Bible affirms that Jesus has already vanquished Satan and the dark army. Even the demons know that Jesus is more powerful than they are. This fact represents assurance to us that we can learn how to align ourselves with Him to defeat these entities. As we move through, we will continue to equip ourselves with all we need to be able to do so.

Demons also know that their days are numbered as we move closer and closer to the appointed end of this time. Neither they nor we know when that day will be. Unlike we who have a future with God, the dark army understands it has no future with God.

THE DARK ARMY EXISTS

Now the Holy Spirit tells us clearly that in the last times some will turn away from the true faith; they will follow deceptive spirits and teachings that come from demons.

1 Timothy 4:1 NLT

You believe that there is one God. Good! Even the demons believe that—and shudder.

James 2:19

So the demons begged, "If you cast us out, send us into that herd of pigs."

Matthew 8:31 NLT

Anyone whom you forgive, I also forgive. Indeed, what I have forgiven, if I have forgiven anything, has been for your sake in the presence of Christ, so that we would not be outwitted by Satan; for we are not ignorant of his designs.

2 Corinthians 2:10–11 ESV

WHAT CAN I DO TODAY?

Acknowledge that you are capable of winning the war for your child in partnership with God. Start by writing the following on an index card and reciting it at every opportunity:

"No weapon formed against you shall prosper, and every tongue which rises against you in judgment you shall condemn."

Isaiah 54:17 NKJV

Dear Lord,
In our time together, I am sharing these challenges concerning my child and declaring, with Your help, that we can defeat the dark army. I know You have a better plan for my child!

1.

2.

3.

PRAYER TO STAND AGAINST THE DARK ARMY

Father, I acknowledge and declare today that the devil and his demons are liars. Thank You for taking the veil off of my spiritual eyes. I agree with Your truth that You are in me and that You are greater than any enemy who attempts to claim my family. As children of the Most High, we are meant to follow Your plans for our lives. Make me brave, Lord, so that I can stand and fight. We are partners in the battle! Help me to learn all I can about the spiritual world—especially as it relates to the freedom and release of my children from the enemy. In Jesus' name, Amen.

A Warrior Parent

I f we believe there is a dark army, then it is necessary that
we clarify who we believe God is today. It may seem like
an indirect place to start, since it feels far from the quick
fix most of us are looking for, but chances are, you already
know deep down that nothing quick and easy is going to
work. Knowing that there is an oppositional force warring
against your children and desiring to know God in a deeper
and more personal way so that you can be a warrior parent
is *step one* of putting your feet solidly on the ground. And
let's face facts. What do we have to lose at this point? Why
not err on the side of God's provision, protection and His
amazing love for us? So, who is God?

God is love. There is not one thing we can do (or not do)
that would make God love us more—or less. He loves us
at our best. He loves us at our worst. When we digest and
embrace this unconditional love, a love that does *not* depend

on our behavior, then we truly can experience a personal relationship with Him. Knowing God, receiving His love for us and understanding that He is fighting our battles for us are the foundational elements that enable us to stand strong against any battle or any army and to believe that victory is on the way!

When we are at war fighting the enemy head-on for our child, we must know our identity. In the middle of trauma or chaos, our identity may seem hidden, lost or possibly not yet discovered. *Step two* is standing strong for as long as it takes.

For years I went to church; however, I had no idea who I was in Christ or how I was to fight evil in the spiritual realm. Seeing ourselves as God sees us and recognizing what He says we are capable of should be the cornerstone of our lives. This knowledge establishes our ability to live in divine assignment and combat our enemy through the confidence of who we are and whose we are in the Kingdom of God.

First and foremost, we must realize that we are children of God. God chose and created us. He does not make mistakes. We are His masterpiece, handmade by Him. Sometimes that can be very hard to see and assimilate. As our children go in directions that we did not anticipate, it is quite natural to blame ourselves. Self-blame is one of the most toxic forms of self-abuse.

We seldom pick just one aspect of our character or actions to over-emphasize. Too often we magnify anything and everything we deem wrong or that is not up to par. Our perceived inadequacies tend only to accomplish one task: They paralyze us. If we remain in a state of self-blame for too long, we can chronically find ways to make whatever occurs in our life seem as though it is our fault. God would never condemn us to this type of existence. All responsibility has already been navigated at the cross. The most healing act we can take is to hand our situation over to Him and concentrate on seeing what is really transpiring.

Taking Responsibility for Ourselves

There is no question that we need to take responsibility for our actions, but we should not be deceived into believing that we are entirely responsible for all that is going on. There are others who are involved with our children—namely the dark army. And there is a healthier way to approach things. First, we should ascertain how far our responsibility extends (the real and true mistakes we have made), and then acknowledge our part and commit to learn from the mistake, correcting our behavior as we move forward. The act of repentance can be defined as recognizing our error, admitting it to God, leaving it at His feet, turning away and moving forward in a better way.

Every father and mother will have doubts about the validity of his or her own parenting skills throughout the growth of the children. It starts almost at birth at the sight of a wee one crying. *Is he wet? Does she have a tummy ache? Is this formula the right one? Is he too cold? Is she too warm? Does he like me? Why can't I fix this?*

Looking back, we can all recognize that this was actually the easiest part of bringing them closer to adulthood. The challenges take on new facets as they get older. By the time a child reaches adolescence, his or her needs have gone way beyond a diaper, cuddle or lullaby.

Parents have the challenge of dealing with the roller-coaster emotional ranges, physical insecurities and more communal tugs that are pulling at their children. That is when we begin to hear accusations like, "Mom, everyone is doing it! Why are you being so mean?" It is no wonder we question ourselves continually. But God appointed us as the stewards of our children. From the start, He created us to take on the identity of *parent*. He believes we are able to make the journey—no matter how hard or easy it may get.

Another key part of our identity in Christ is that we are soldiers in God's army. God is our general. The day that we acknowledged Jesus Christ as our Lord and Savior and repented for our sins was our enlistment day. Our sole role as a soldier is to counter evil and fight for the Lord's Kingdom— not physically, but spiritually.

There is a truth we must face right now. We cannot avoid facing spiritual pressures from the dark army for the rest of our natural lives. But then, what are the consequences of completely ignoring our partnership with God? During previous wars, there were some who elected to avoid war completely. Many were punished with fines and incarceration. What if we should decide to opt for a draft evasion and attempt to elude our spiritual enlistment? If we do, we risk experiencing spiritual occurrences that could drastically affect our futures. At the moment of our separation from God, we become spiritually exposed and are without His protection.

Both the light and dark armies will continue to exist whether we participate or not. When we disobey God, which is what a draft dodger does, Satan becomes aware. That makes us a target-rich environment. We can expect to see more and more invasion from the devil and his demons. The costliest outcome stems from the fact that all sin is punishable by death. We have no way of overcoming this except through Jesus. This would be an extremely unwise option. Walking away does not ensure that the dark army will leave us alone. In fact, it almost ensures greater attention.

God Supplies Our Armor

The Bible tells us to fight the good fight of faith (see 1 Timothy 6:12). But how do we do that? It is God who gives us the weapons to protect ourselves and to successfully fight. He explains that we are to put on the armor with which He has endowed us. "Finally, be strong in the Lord and in his mighty power. Put on the full armor of God, so that you can take your stand against the devil's schemes" (Ephesians 6:10–11). Armor, in an overall sense, is a covering used to protect an object or an individual from physical injury or damage. It is useful to protect against direct contact weapons or projectiles during combat. I think we can agree that armor is great to have around for potentially dangerous environments or activities.

A knight's uniform is an easily recognized example of armor. While the components of spiritual armor can be compared to physical uniforms, they take on so much more in meaning. To begin with, we put on the full armor of God as our committed expression of trust in God and what He has done for us through Jesus. Even though the following explanation may seem symbolic, it is not. Each piece requires an action and belief. We have to embrace each in order for them to work.

Another aspect of spiritual armor is that we may not immediately see its impact. It is much like when we water a tiny seed that has been planted in a bit of soil. At the time, we have no idea what the end product will look like. It takes a full-blooming tomato plant to bear much fruit. In His timing, God makes us aware of what is being accomplished, and all along there are processes taking place that we will never see. Let's take a look at the individual pieces of armor and how they serve us.

Armor starts with the top of our body—our head—as it should. This complex organ controls our thoughts, memory, emotions, motor skills, vision, breathing and more. It regulates every process that transpires in our bodies. In the Roman era or biblical times, a helmet provided protection by assembling layers of thick leather or brass to keep a blow to the head from causing fatal injuries.

In the spiritual realm, our helmet is that of God-given salvation. Today's dictionary defines *salvation* as "protecting somebody from danger, disaster or loss."[1] A believer's definition for *salvation* is "the state of being saved from the power of evil, salvation from sin."[2] This is brought about by faith in Christ.

As we battle for our children against Satan, we may indeed get hurt, but we can take refuge in knowing that God has removed any chance of fatality. He has already supplied us with eternal life that continues after we leave this earth. We cannot be destroyed by evil. Even if we fall or are wounded, we will not lose the battle while we are wearing His helmet.

A soldier's belt should keep his clothes from falling down or moving out of position on his body. The placement of each article of armor is critical. The spiritual belt of truth is the availability and our familiarity of God's Word and His promises. The action ensconced in attiring ourselves with the belt of truth is not only our commitment to study and learn as much about God as we possibly can, but also to continue to chase that knowledge for the rest of our natural lives.

When we put God's Word into our hearts, we can use it freely to defeat Satan's attacks. The more familiar we are with God's promises, the easier it is for those promises to bubble up and out of our spirit in time of great need. The Word of God provides direction, answered prayer, strength, instruction, conviction and correction. It is yet another tool we use to grow in awareness of both God's identity and ours.

As our children are making self-destructive choices and defying our guidance, we will often silently entertain many defeating thoughts that float through our minds. *This is never going to be over. I can't stand to watch this anymore. I am helpless and don't know what to do about it. Where is God when you need Him?* We cannot afford to listen to the lies spit out by the enemy camp. We have to keep the belt of truth fastened tightly around us at all times so that the Word of God and His truth are easy to retrieve. We cannot fall prey to the attempts of the dark army to discourage and disappoint us to the point that we are willing to quit fighting for our children.

It helps to keep several key Scripture passages from the living and breathing Word of God close. We can write them on our bathroom mirror, carry the index cards we have been working on or purchase encouraging artwork to hang on the walls of our homes. It is worth the time to designate our favorites—and the most inspiring—and surround ourselves with them.

Next, a soldier would don a breastplate to cover his body from the neck to the thighs. The most crucial protection a breastplate provided was to keep the heart covered. The heart is the focus of both our physical and spiritual well-being. It is often the symbol for love due to its compassion, understanding and care capabilities. The spiritual breastplate of righteousness protects our hearts from sin, discouragement and disappointment.

In other words, the breastplate keeps us from becoming hard-hearted. A hardened heart is one that is unmoved by things about which others would feel compassion. Even more than the lack of emotion, it also represents rebellion against

God. "The good person out of the good treasure of his heart produces good, and the evil person out of his evil treasure produces evil, for out of the abundance of the heart his mouth speaks" (Luke 6:45 ESV). Our breastplate reminds us continually that we are in right standing with God—our partner—and that we can live inside His will and power.

Satan strives to break our hearts. His goal is to make us feel as if our children will never find freedom from the darkness. That is why it is necessary to guard our hearts by spiritually putting on this breastplate. We do not want to lose hope along the way. As long as we are in partnership with God, we can expect Him to come through on behalf of our children. The breastplate works in coordination with all our spiritual armor. Let's investigate the rest.

Another element of spiritual armor are the shoes of peace. Think about the different types of shoes we have in our closets. There are the fuzzy slippers we wear around the house. They are so much more comfortable than the dress shoes we slide on to go to special events. Then there are the everyday shoes. These are the work shoes that enable us to accomplish eight to ten hours of wear without blisters or throbbing. And we must not forget the athletic wear. Everyone has a favorite pair that they use for walking, jogging or hiking. Nowadays when an army goes forth, they are generally outfitted in combat boots. But when the Roman army wore sandals, they were signifying that they were ready for battle. Their sandals had nails that gripped the ground to establish surefootedness.

Our spiritual equivalent is in stark contrast to those sandals. We are given shoes of peace. These shoes equip us to walk through enemy attacks guided by peace that is powered by Jesus. Our shoes are fitted with the good news of the Gospel and with the assurance that Jesus will help us walk through the fiery trials of our lives. Spiritual peace is a state of wholeness and completeness that can take on immunity to surrounding circumstances. It is a physical and spiritual calm that remains, regardless of what is going on around us. As we stride forward in the shoes of peace, we are able to think clearly and respond appropriately and calmly to the end God intends, no matter what is transpiring.

All Roman soldiers were issued a shield. It was oblong and was strapped to the soldier's arm. It was designed to be held above the head or straight out to deflect the flaming darts of their enemies. Our spiritual shield is comprised of faith. It announces both that we are trusting God regardless of what we face from the enemy and that we know in our hearts that He loves us.

During times of stress, it can seem as though all the faith we have accumulated has evaporated in a mist. Not so. We always have a measure of faith whether we feel it or not. And furthermore, we can increase that measure in a very simple way: Pray for more and believe you have received it. The core component in wielding the shield of faith is a simple belief that all of God's promises are meant for all His people. Most importantly, carrying the shield of faith is evidence—whether we see it yet or not—that our victory is coming. Satan throws all kinds of fiery darts our way as we fight to win our children back; therefore, we must take the shield of faith very seriously.

Rest and recovery also reside behind this shield. It is estimated that one in three adults do not get enough sleep on a regular basis. The more serious issues connected to sleep deprivation include high blood pressure, diabetes, heart attack or stroke. The minor concerns are not much better. They include obesity, depression and more.[3] It makes sense that fatigue leads to a lowering of our alertness and concentration levels. This fact alone lets us know that our abilities to logically think through things, perform tasks or even pray can be hindered. The shield of faith can provide the space we need to recoup our energy and prayer lives.

The last weapon and the sixth piece of God's armor is the sword of the Spirit. The Word of God is our sword. We must use God's words—those we have accumulated through the belt of truth—to defend ourselves and our family. We can do that by clinging daily to our Bible and allowing God to speak to us, comfort us and reveal to us what He desires to divulge. The sword of the Spirit turns us into victors and not victims. By seizing the Word and speaking His promises aloud to the enemy, we can find a new level of boldness. This is imperative as we prepare to run the dark army out of our lives.

Understanding who we are in Christ and putting on the armor of God daily will keep us *ahead* of our enemy. When we stand with God as His soldiers, we become fully equipped for each and every battle. We gain the assurance of knowing how to fight as a Christ-follower and a warrior-parent who will never consider losing. History has shown that any war can be won if we focus on our strengths and if we capitalize on the weaknesses of the opponent. Jesus is our strength. He is Satan's weakness. While it is likely we may lose certain battles to win the overall war, we must be patient and continue to partner with God. Sooner or later, we will see victory!

AN IDENTITY EXERCISE

Fill in the blanks:

▸ I am made in _____ image (see Genesis 1:27).

▸ I am a child of _____ (see John 1:12).

- ▸ I belong to _____ (see 1 Corinthians 6:20).
- ▸ I have been _____ before the world was created (see Ephesians 1:4).
- ▸ I am _____ as Your child (see Ephesians 1:5).
- ▸ I am a _____ of heaven (see Philippians 3:20).
- ▸ I have been given _____ (see 1 Corinthians 15:57).

WHAT CAN I DO TODAY?

Familiarize yourself with your full spiritual armor by writing on your index card what each piece of armor can do for you.

Helmet of Salvation, Belt of Truth, Breastplate of Righteousness, Shoes of Peace, Shield of Faith and Sword of the Spirit.

IDENTITY AND ARMOR PRAYER

Father, I pray that You would open the eyes of my heart so that I may be fully aware of my identity in You. Help me to see myself as You see me. Thank You for providing the armor I need to do battle with You for my family. I ask that You help me stay committed to putting on Your armor daily. I intend to continue to learn and grow in You to contribute to the well-being of myself, my spouse and my children. In Jesus' name, Amen.

5

We Have Tremendous Authority

The more we understand about how much God is on our side and how He has bestowed power within us, the easier it becomes to be prayer warriors for our children. This process begins by gaining knowledge about our authority.

When a boss walks into the office, he expects to have his instructions, orders and rules followed. We have seen both good bosses and not-so-good bosses. Each has a distinctive set of traits. When describing the not-so-good, we often hear comments such as *disrespect, shirking responsibility, wasting time* and *negative environment*. The good boss list is in stark contrast. We hear phrases such as *takes charge, values others, is respectful* and *fosters positivity.*

Learning about and executing our spiritual authority is a lot like training to be a good boss. By functioning within the will of God, we are guaranteed not to overstep our boundaries the way a not-so-good boss (or the leader of the dark army) does consistently. When I became aware of the good authority given to me by God, my battle strategy on behalf of my children changed. You have the good authority, as well!

Jesus explained to us how we *all* currently possess complete authority over everything—both in the earth and over the earth. "Look, I have given you authority over all the power of the enemy" (Luke 10:19 NLT). It is amazing that when we confessed our sins and made the Lord our Savior, we were delivered from the devil. We entered into a position of authority through Jesus Christ as the sons and daughters of the Living God.

If you have not taken Jesus into your heart, confessed your sins and asked Him to wash you clean, then I encourage you to make Him the Lord of your life. Do it right now! This is the only way to access your authority. Receiving the love of God, along with allowing Jesus to wash your sins away and make you white as snow, gives you all that you need to stomp on the devil's head and defeat evil.

Just in case you need it, here is a prayer of salvation. Remember, after you recite it, you can consider yourself a member of God's army.

> *Lord Jesus, I confess that I have sinned, and I ask for Your forgiveness. Please come into my heart and become my Lord and Savior. Help me to partner with You through the Holy Spirit. Thank You for dying on the cross for my sins and for giving me eternal life with You in heaven. In Jesus' name I pray, Amen.*

Having authority that moves through the power of God is huge. It gives us the capacity and potential to bring dead things back to life. We have the power to heal the sick. Most importantly, we have the power to stand against the dark army in protection of ourselves and our children. God has given us everything we need to achieve victory over the devil's destructive work.

In the previous chapter, we learned that we have armor that was given to us by God, and we are meant to put it on daily. When the Roman soldiers put on their armor, they did not simply put on their gear and then stand waiting. The armor and weapons are at our disposal, but we have to be proactive. We should not simply pray and ask God to fight our battles for us. That is not how any partnership works. Through the power of the Holy Spirit and the name of Jesus, we can speak directly to the devil and stand firm within God's power. We can take qualified actions and change our behavior with confidence. The devil has to flee in the face of God's armor.

Areas of Authority

There are several definitions of authority that are expressed scripturally. Luke 10:19, which we discussed above, also says that you have authority to "trample on snakes and scorpions and to overcome all the power of the enemy." Isaiah 54:17 assures that "no weapon forged against you will prevail." The book of Ephesians declares your authority by saying that because you are in Christ, "God placed all things under his feet and appointed him to be head over everything" (1:22). This verse describes the transference of power to you through Jesus.

The pivot point for me was recognizing that everything really did mean *everything*, including all the tools and defenses necessary to defeat the devil and his attacks. But it is important to note that God has given us *the choice* as to whether or not we will repent, make Jesus our Savior and become filled with His power (called the Holy Spirit).

Once we know that we have power and authority over the devil, we must stay diligent. In our home, we fought close to a hundred battles during the fifteen years we wrestled with the dark army before we saw complete deliverance in our children.

Even though it is our greatest weapon, the act of taking authority sometimes contains seasons when it is hard to see any results. Many times, the answers we receive do not resemble what we requested of God. In the midst of the battle, we often have to depend solely on our spiritual eyes to see the blessings within our circumstances. We must persevere with our prayers and never lean on our own understanding of how they might manifest.

A Look at Daniel

Let's dig into a story from the Bible that can be found in the book of Daniel (see 10:2–3, 12–13). Here we meet a man, Daniel, who was crying out to God with a desperate plea on behalf of his nation. The nation of Judah had come under judgment from God. For seventy years (an entire generation) his people had been held in captivity by their enemy, the Babylonians. God had repeatedly warned the nation to clean up its act, but the people never repented. Daniel was desperate for his people to be delivered, and God allowed him to warn them. He glorified God in all that he did, and because of that devotion, he was being threatened with death. Still, he would not bow down to any other authority. He chose instead to ignore his circumstances and plead with God.

Daniel fasted and prayed. He did not eat for 21 days. Then the angel Gabriel came to Daniel. God's angel told him that from the very first day that Daniel had set his heart to pray for deliverance, his words had been heard. That is such a comforting thing to know; however, we should also learn from the fact that for 21 days the demons in charge of Persia prevented Gabriel from visiting Daniel. In fact, it was not until the archangel Michael came to help that Gabriel broke through the stronghold.

Now that is spiritual warfare. Daniel was an ordinary human, just like we are. Because of this, we know he must have become weary quickly. Have we not all been there? Nevertheless, the story shows us that if we do not lose faith and if we persevere, God is faithful to answer and deliver us!

Even Jesus Was Tempted

The truth that has had the greatest impact on me was realizing that Jesus knows about Satan's power of temptation and how it makes us feel. The primary reason He can comfort us in the battlefield is because He knows what it is like to battle one-on-one with the devil. The best pattern of a warfare prayer that we can use to combat the powers of darkness can be taken from Jesus Himself.

As we read through Matthew 4:1–11, we see that Jesus, the Son of God and Son of mankind, was tempted for forty days in the desert by the devil. Jesus was tired, weak and hungry, as we would be. It is good to remember that the devil will always slither into our lives and present the greatest temptations when we are at our lowest. So it was with Jesus. He was tempted in every way. We can follow His success over the devil's attack.

First, Satan tempted Jesus with food. Jesus was fasting. In fact, He fasted for forty straight days. Another good question to ask ourselves is how long we would last in the same situation. The devil said, "If you are the Son of God, tell these stones to become bread" (verse 3).

In today's terms, the temptation would be to do what feels right or to submit to the lust of the flesh. *Go ahead and get the triple-meat burger and super-size the fries. Who is going to know?* If you are feeling sad, the temptation could be different. *Surely it's okay to stop by the bar and have a couple of drinks to take the edge off my misery.*

When the devil approached Jesus, he knew it was all about appealing to His human, fleshly desires. But Jesus showed us the correct way to respond to this type of temptation. His reply to the devil was, "Man shall not live on bread alone, but on every word that comes from the mouth of God" (verse 4).

Jesus could have easily changed the stones to bread, but He did not want to satisfy any temptation through His divine power. He chose to act out of the will of His Father. Jesus knew how to trust God. He also believed that the Word of God is living bread. When we are fighting for our children and are at our lowest point, we always will have God's Word. As we feast on the words of God, we are protected and given provision. Learning to trust God in a greater way strengthens us.

Next, Satan chose to tempt Jesus with the pride of life. In other words, he wanted Jesus to act out of His own will and not God's. Satan took Jesus to the holy city and tempted Him to show off. "Then the devil took him to the holy city and had him stand on the highest point of the temple. 'If you are the Son of God,' he said, 'throw yourself down'" (verses 5–6).

There will be many times when we are tempted to execute shortcuts for our children. Those paths, however, may not be God's best answer for them. If we intervene, we can shortcut the tests of life that God has orchestrated for our children. There are difficulties our children need to face that will determine His best outcomes for them. If Jesus had failed to overcome this temptation, He would have started His ministry apart from God's direction.

Making life easier for our children is second nature. When they are small and helpless, we understand intuitively that we have to be their hands and feet. But if we continue in that vein, bringing them whatever they desire or need at their beck and call, they will never have a reason to learn to walk or run. Jesus shows us how unwise it is to get ahead of God. If we read further, we know that Jesus answered Satan by saying, "It is also written: 'Do not put the Lord your God to the test'" (verse 7).

When we are tempted to bow down to what we want—or what our kids are crying for—in order to shorten a process, everyone loses. This wonderful example, displayed by Jesus, is a great reminder to humbly stay in the presence of God. By laying ourselves and our children down at His throne where His will and power can be realized, we can feed positively into the destiny and future of our children.

The last temptation of Jesus can be termed *lust of the eyes*. Satan makes one last effort to tempt Jesus. "Again, the devil took him to a very high mountain and showed him all the kingdoms of the world and their splendor. 'All this I will give you,' he said, 'if you will bow down and worship me'" (verses 8–9). Satan wanted to alter the allegiance of Jesus to worship him and not God, His Father. Had He agreed, this would have taken God's perfect plans to hell.

Jesus could have chosen to fall into this temptation of selfishness. He could have bypassed the pain of the cross and forgotten about all of us. But Jesus rebuked Satan, saying, "Away from me, Satan! For it is written: 'Worship the Lord your God, and serve him only'" (verse 10). He *defeated successfully* Satan by resisting the temptation to control everything and bow down to evil. When we are tired and the battle seems long, we must follow the vital step of bowing down at God's feet and allowing Him control over everything.

As we read about this battle between Satan and Jesus, we can learn so much. When we are battle weary while fighting for the lives of our children, it is normal to become weak and tired, just as Jesus was in the desert. We can take heart and emulate Him by staying in God's Word, which keeps us strong and full of hope. We must act on God's will for our lives and our children's lives so that we do not test God's plans. We must relinquish control and allow God to move both them and us through our brokenness. God has a plan and purpose for everyone.

Though others may join us in praying for our children, no one else can pray for them as we can. We are in a spiritual war for our children's lives that translates as good versus evil. The enemy is out to steal, kill and destroy our children. But Jesus came to deliver us and heal the brokenhearted so that we can live a life of abundance (see John 10:10). Prayer that is coupled with knowledge of authority is the ultimate weapon when we are battling for our children's lives. We can take our authority over the devil and stomp on his evil head.

Do not be afraid to respond to the devil with a resounding no. Remember that we have the added protection of our spiritual armor. Speak it out loud if you need to. Shout it if it feels better to do that. If your spirit warns you against an action or an individual, take heed. Consider what is at stake. So many times we think about occurrences as being fleeting and short-lived, but some can be life altering. Looking back, I can recall singular moments when my children's lives were in the balance merely over the company they sought out. The Holy Spirit was there to sound the alarm, but at the time, I did not have the ears to hear and respond. Cultivate your spiritual eyes and ears and turn them in the direction of what your children are chasing.

Ask God what it is He requires of you, tell Him your deepest fears and cry with Him over your children. He is a bigger God than anything you face. He can bear any and all of your burdens; furthermore, He wants you to share them. Always be assured that your prayers are heard from the moment they are spoken, collected in a heavenly cistern and awaiting their release in God's timing. Battlefield prayers are premiere weapons to winning the battle over darkness and delivering our children from evil.

If You Are Considering Fasting

Fasting is a spiritual discipline that is practiced in order to develop spiritual strength, including resisting temptation. It is a preferred way to build our inner man because, by denying ourselves pleasure, the Holy Spirit moves in His strength and helps us deny our fleshly desires. It is like working our physical muscles. As we begin weight lifting, we start off with the lightest weights available. Then, as our muscles become stronger, we can increase our resistance and build bigger muscles.

Fasting can create an opportunity to become aware of the supernatural power that enables us to live more like Jesus. Then we begin to hear, touch, see, feel and experience God in a much deeper way than ever before.

There is no set period of time in which we should set aside items in our lives, but we must *always* keep health and safety in mind (in regard to severity of food and drink limitations and of lengths of time). Fasting practices are traditionally broken down into *short, intermittent* and *extended*.

SEVERAL ITEMS THAT CAN BE USED TO BEGIN A FASTING DISCIPLINE

1. Splurge foods and drinks such as soda, coffee, chocolate or other indulgences
2. Naps exchanged for Bible study
3. Surfing the internet or social media
4. Television time exchanged for prayer time
5. Skipping one meal daily

WHAT CAN I DO TODAY?

The only way to be purposeful about prayer is to integrate it into your schedule as you would eating your daily meals. Decide what your personal prayer schedule should look like and record those time blocks in your calendar.

Write out this Scripture verse on an index card to remind you of the importance of committed prayer. "Rejoice always, pray without ceasing, give thanks in all circumstances; for this is the will of God in Christ Jesus for you" (1 Thessalonians 5:16–18 ESV).

A PRAYER OF AUTHORITY

Father, thank You for giving us full authority over Satan and his dark army. Thank You that You have given us over 7,000 promises in Your Bible. I claim all of them for myself and my family. Today, I commit to a steady and consistent prayer life that will enable me to build an intimate relationship with You. You are my source of all things good, and I will follow You all the days of my life! In Jesus' name, Amen.

PART TWO

TOOLS FOR BATTLE

Prayers—Our Winning Weapons

s we have learned, prayer is an essential element for plugging into the type of power that is an absolute necessity to save our children. But there is another thing to consider.

Picture the two of us sitting across from each other. I would like to pose a question: If you are not protecting your children, no matter their age, then who will do it? Our prayers function as the superior defensive weapon against the devil's darts that are thrown at our children. This life-saving wisdom was downloaded to me by God through prayer. It would prove to be the only thing that suppressed the enemy and spared my children's lives. There is one specific prayer that represents the prayer of all prayers. Let's look closely at what it entails.

Our First Prayer Weapon

Our first prayer weapon is to plead the blood of Jesus over our children as soon as they are born. But, maybe, like me, no one has ever taught you to do this. I had been told to pray to God, and I knew I was supposed to pray for my children's futures. Our daughter, Kaylee, started out needing lots of prayer. We had been on our knees many times asking Him to heal her from certain death because of health issues, but we had never been taught about praying the blood of Jesus over our kids. I believe it made a huge difference in their eventual successful futures.

Pleading the blood of Jesus is an older term that was heard quite often back in the day. When you plead the blood of Jesus over an individual, you are asking for the power of Christ to work within any and every problem. It is a symbolic term that recognizes and acknowledges that the blood shed by Christ on the cross now covers all who believe in Him.

Many of us have not been taught about the actual power of Jesus' blood and its importance. The blood of Jesus is the *only* defense against Satan and his demons. Jesus died on the cross for all our sins—in their entirety. His act included the sins we committed yesterday, the ones we commit today and the ones we will commit in the future. This is when God reconciled all of us to Himself—even the greatest of sinners. "The law requires that nearly everything be cleansed with blood, and without the shedding of blood there is no forgiveness" (Hebrews 9:22).

The blood of Jesus is also the power source for life and victory over darkness. The power from His blood will never run out. When we mix our testimony of overcoming with the blood of Jesus, we are guaranteed to defeat the enemy. "They triumphed over him by the blood of the Lamb and by the word of their testimony" (Revelation 12:11). When you plead the blood of Jesus, you are announcing that your child belongs to and is protected by God.

So how does it work on a practical level? How did I accomplish this spiritual task? First, I visualized Jesus on the cross dying and bleeding. I could see His blood dropping down from the thorny crown that had been placed upon His head and was digging into His flesh. I could envision his blood-soaked hands and feet where the nails had been placed.

From that point, I took His blood, figuratively, and loaded up an imaginary paintbrush. While they slept, I brushed my children's backs in a downward stroke. Then, I took the blood-soaked brush and moved it horizontally across their shoulders. With that imaginary, blood-soaked brush I formed a cross on the backs and arms of my children.

I said aloud, "God, as certain as Jesus died on the cross for all sinners, I cover my child, Steven. Father, he is Your child, and in the name of Jesus and by the power of His blood, I pray protection and wisdom over him." I made sure to announce their names, one by one, Steven, Lawson and Kaylee, and go through the process three separate times.

I revisited this cross-making, blood-soaked paintbrush prayer over and over. I did this not because I did not believe that He heard me the first time, but because I knew that God loves perseverance. The continuous paintbrush strokes demonstrated my faith in Him. It would encourage me and fuel the fight for my children, even when I could not see how they would ever find victory. It was a habit that I knew would be an integral part in winning the battle with Satan over my children.

There were times when I would cry out to God in great despair, especially as one of my children faced tremendous trials and the consequences of self-destructive choices. I continued to draw these blood crosses upon the backs of my children while they remained under attack by the devil.

Every time I went through my ritual, I was reminded that my children belonged to God and that they were only on loan to me. They were His creations, and He cared more for them than I did. It was my way of reassuring myself and bolstering my faith enough to face another day.

We Must Not Give Up

Full disclosure: there were times I almost gave up. I doubted that these cross prayers were working. I came close to the false belief that neither God nor I was doing anything valid to help my children. We must never fall for these lies. The greatest hope that we can possess is to believe that every prayer is heard by God. Always. The Bible clearly tells us this truth. "If you believe, you will receive whatever you ask for in prayer" (Matthew 21:22).

To prove this fact to me, God gave me a vision on one of my darkest days. I saw a large, bronze cistern that was located in heaven. It was overflowing with what appeared to be words. Then it occurred to me that those were the words of my prayers that I had sent to Him so many times when I was in a deep pit of devastation, despair and crying out. These words represented my hope that God would turn things around and make them right. It took me a while to realize the full content of what I had seen. God is collecting all of our prayers in heavenly cisterns. The power within them is being realized. They are kept until God's perfectly timed answer is delivered.

I experienced one example of this truth when Lawson started hanging out with a kid who I knew was bad news. His new friend was a troubled teen who was greatly influencing my son in a terrible way. At sixteen, Lawson became ill. Because he had previously battled with life-threatening sepsis at age nine, we always monitored any mosquito bites or wounds to make sure they were not getting infected.

That afternoon, he went to my husband, Steve, and had him look at his elbow. His dad suggested they go to the doctor. I was the one who received a phone call letting me know that Lawson was being admitted into the hospital with a septic elbow. I was in Denver, Colorado, at the time taking care of Kaylee, who was having a lung biopsy. I thought, *How could two of my children be states apart and both be in serious condition? Where is God in all of this?*

I thought that this additional emergency was a poorly timed allowance by God; however, I learned later that Lawson's new friend had been arrested for grand larceny. If Lawson had not been admitted to the hospital on the exact day and at the exact hour that he was, then he would have most certainly been in the car with this new friend. These events that occurred simultaneously did not make sense to me at first, but when I realized the significance, they changed my perspective.

This was where the enemy was steering Lawson's life. He would have gone to jail at sixteen for being an accessory to stealing property that was valued in the thousands of dollars. This troubled teen had stolen the merchandise and items before he had met Lawson, and he kept the goods in his trunk. Lawson would have never known; but because he would have been in the car, he would have been incarcerated, too!

I believe with all my heart that God used that infection in Lawson's body to save him from a life-altering brush with the law that would have had an impact on Lawson's life forever. I believe that my prayers were activated and initiated on the day I prayed them, but they were answered in a way I would have never asked. There is power in praying the blood of Jesus over your children.

In Exodus we find an example of placing and pleading the blood of Jesus. "The blood on your doorposts will serve as a sign, marking the houses where you are staying. When I see the blood, I will pass over you. This plague of death will not touch you when I strike the land of Egypt" (Exodus 12:13 NLT). The story around this verse started when the Pharaoh of Egypt kept the children of Israel as slaves to do his bidding. They worked as masons and stonecutters to build the pyramids and great cities. They were even tasked with building roads.

But many years earlier, God had promised Abraham that a time of freedom would come. That promise, however, was not on Pharaoh's mind. So God sent Moses to win their freedom. When Pharaoh ignored his pleas, God sent a series of plagues to the land that included lots of nasty stuff like water turning into blood, frogs, lice, gnats, diseased livestock, boils, hail, locusts and utter darkness for three days. The Israelites were still expecting freedom and were intent on escaping Pharaoh, but it did not happen until the tenth and final plague was executed. The plague included the angel of death passing through the land of Egypt and striking down the firstborn son of every household.

To protect the Israelites, God instructed them to mark their doors with the blood of a sacrificed lamb. They were to stay behind that closed door. This was a Passover offering so that God would pass over their homes, which spared all firstborns within. When the angel of death came through Egypt and saw the lamb's blood on the tops and sides of the door frames of the Israeli homes, God did not allow the destroyer to enter.

This is exactly what occurs around our prayers today. When we plead the blood of Jesus, we are literally and figuratively placing the blood of Jesus upon the frames of our children's hearts and lives. We are covering them so that when the enemy tries to gain entrance into their lives to kill them, he will be denied. He cannot get in because they are covered by the powerful blood of Jesus!

Other Forms of Prayers

We can also use a second type of prayer that involves reading God's Word and praying it back to Him. In specific battles, I would take a verse like Psalm 40:1, "I waited patiently for the LORD; he turned to me and heard my cry," and I would remind God that I was patiently waiting on Him and was expecting Him to turn my way as He heard my cries. This would be my prayer: *God, I am reminding You of my patience, and I know that You will help me as You hear my cries.* It was very reassuring to pray His Word during my darkest moments.

I did not know the true value of speaking over my own or my children's lives until I began to speak Psalm 91 aloud over them, personalizing the passage by placing our names within the verses. The peace that would flow over me as I began to say these passages aloud (and while I believed them with all my heart) was life-transforming and fueled me to continue to pray victory for my children.

Perhaps in your study time, you will find a verse that resonates with you. Do not hesitate to personalize it and speak it out. Over time, you may feel led to shift to another verse or add it to the verses you are already using. What you choose to plead over your children is up to you and God.

There are so many other things to pray for concerning our children. Every topic introduces another weapon against the dark army. Let's explore just a few. We can add more topics as we see the need. In your imagination, place your children at the feet of Jesus so that He can lay His capable hands upon them.

1. We can pray for godly wisdom to activate in the lives of our children. This provides the capacity for our children to make good decisions and keep their future in focus. We know that every decision they make will have an impact on them in some way. They may not be at a place yet to pray this for themselves, so we must stand in the gap and do it for them. The Bible says that the only way to get wisdom from God is to ask for it. It is amazing how many times we overlook this simple verse that is full of very helpful instruction. "If any of you lacks wisdom, you should ask God, who gives generously to all without finding fault, and it will be given to you" (James 1:5).

2. We can pray concerning our children's friends and the company they choose to keep. Our children often mingle with individuals we never have the opportunity to meet.

3. We can ask God to surround them with angels that will ward off anyone who means to do them harm.

4. We can pray for them to meet and form friendships that provide healthy spiritual growth.

5. We can ask God to send mentors and teachers into their paths whom they can respect and learn from.

6. We can ask that God would give them help to navigate the stresses that exist in their lives in ways that glorify Him.

7. We can pray that He comforts them and creates safe places and people with whom they can voice their concerns—above and beyond their parents.

In the heat of the battle, it can be difficult to see or keep track of any progress our children have made inside their challenges. It is important to remember and take note of anything and everything. That is why a prayer journal (notebook of any type) is also a good investment. Although there is considerable value in speaking prayers over our children, a journal provides a place to record our daily prayers and the answers that follow.

We can begin our entries by recalling, with gratitude, the blessings we see in our lives that God has been gracious to provide. After that, we can list our specific prayer requests. The key word is *specific*. We want our children whole, healthy and thriving, but how? I wrote down small victories such as, *Steven came home on time tonight and seemed sober.* Then, I would thank God by writing out a prayer in the journal. I logged in these small acts of obedience. Many times reflecting on these small journal entries would be the exact encouragement I needed to keep believing that God was still turning things around.

Feel free to use the space to scribble notes to God, as well as any distinct instructions or revelations you receive that you need to remember. I flip back through my journal frequently. A prayer journal creates a written history with God that can inspire and encourage us over time.

SCRIPTURE TO SPEAK OVER YOUR CHILDREN AS YOU PRAY

Nothing can separate our children from God:

> For I am convinced that neither death nor life, neither angels nor demons, neither the present nor the future, nor any powers, neither height nor depth, nor anything else in all creation,

will be able to separate us from the love of God that is in Christ Jesus our Lord.

Romans 8:38–39

No scheme of the enemy perpetrated on our children will succeed:

"No weapon formed against you will succeed, and you will refute any accusation raised against you in court. This is the heritage of the Lord's servants, and their righteousness is from Me." This is the Lord's declaration.

Isaiah 54:17 HCSB

Our households will be saved:

So they said, "Believe on the Lord Jesus Christ, and you will be saved, you and your household."

Acts 16:31 NKJV

God is committed to saving our children:

Shall the prey be taken from the mighty, or the captives of the righteous be delivered? But thus says the Lord: "Even the captives of the mighty shall be taken away, and the prey of the terrible be delivered; for I will contend with him who contends with you, and I will save your children."

Isaiah 49:24–25 NKJV

We can take authority in the name of Jesus so that our children know their identity in Him:

"Do not be afraid of those who kill the body but cannot kill the soul. Rather, be afraid of the One who can destroy both soul and body in hell. Are not two sparrows sold for a penny? Yet not one of them will fall to the ground outside your Father's care. And even the very hairs of your head are all numbered. So don't be afraid; you are worth more than many sparrows."

Matthew 10:28–31

Angels surround our children:

> "Beware that you don't look down on any of these little ones. For
> I tell you that in heaven their angels are always in the presence
> of my heavenly Father."

Matthew 18:10 NLT

 ## WHAT CAN I DO TODAY?

Please put your name and the names of your children and your
family in the blanks below:

_____ who dwells in the shelter
of the Most High will abide in the shadow of the Almighty.
_____ will say to the LORD, "My refuge and
my fortress, my God in whom I trust." For he will deliver
_____ from the snare of the fowler and from
the deadly pestilence. He will cover _____
with his pinions, and under his wings _____
will find refuge; his faithfulness is a shield and buckler.
_____ will not feel the terror of the night, nor
the arrow that flies by day, nor the pestilence that stalks in
darkness, nor the destruction that wastes at noonday. A thousand may fall at _____'s side, ten thousand
at _____'s right hand, but it will not come near
_____. _____ will only look
with [his/her] eyes and see the recompense of the wicked.
Because _____ [has] made the LORD [his/her]
dwelling place—the Most High, who is _____'s
refuge—no evil shall be allowed to befall _____,
no plague come near _____'s tent. For he
will command his angels concerning _____
to guard _____ in all [his/her] ways.
On their hands they will bear _____ up,
lest _____ strike [his/her] foot against a
stone. _____ will tread on the lion and adder;
the young lion and serpent [he/she] will trample underfoot.

"Because _____ holds fast to me in love, I will deliver [him/her]; I will protect _____, because _____ knows my name. When _____calls to me, I will answer [him/her]; I will be with _____ in trouble; I will rescue _____ and honor [him/her]. With long life I will satisfy _____ and show [him/her] my salvation."

Psalm 91 ESV

A PRAYER ON PRAYER

Father, thank You for helping me to realize how precious the blood that Your Son shed on the cross is to my life and that of my family. I plead His blood over my entire family and declare them Yours. I celebrate that Your power and His wonderful blood are working on our behalf every single day! I will continue to pray over my children every day and ask for Your instruction as to what to pray for in relation to conquering the enemy. In Jesus' name, Amen.

In the Meantime

As we call upon God and wait for His answer, we will go through the Meantime Phase (which is what happens between the *amen* and the *answer*). It is the indeterminate period before something happens or before a specified period ends. It is the amount of time we spend navigating a situation until something else occurs and we can turn the page of life and get on with it.

If we are not careful during these Meantime Phases, we can easily get caught up in the schemes, lies and strategies of the enemy. We may find ourselves faltering under the weight of added burdens beyond the physical, such as the bombardment of thoughts of unbelief, bursts of hopelessness and the angst of defeat. These battles are painful and are just as real as anything else that might be going on before our eyes. You can, however, successfully navigate a Meantime Phase (no matter how long) by developing three coping tools: patience, perseverance and altered perspective. I like to call them the Three Ps.

Patience

This will come as no surprise, but nurturing patience can be the hardest part of the journey. When life is good and things are going our way, patience seems almost effortless—because we have little need of it.

But when situations are raging regarding our children and we want or need them to be rescued *now*, it can seem almost impossible to find a thread of patience. And then apply it? That is a big ask in any situation. In fact, it might seem much easier to pull out our hair.

The emotions and thoughts raging through our parental minds demonstrate just about everything but patience. *I had no idea parenting could be this difficult! If you only knew how much I'd like to take you over my knee . . . even if you are sixteen! What will it take before you gain enough maturity and good sense to see what you are doing to yourself and your family? Another crazy idea? How many do you have in your teen head? God, where are You?*

It takes only one impulsive slip, and our words are out there hanging in the air (and in our children's ears), serving to further stoke an already raging fire. In chaotic and dark circumstances, patience is often the hardest but most necessary choice within our good options.

One of the key elements I learned about patience is that it is a controlled action, unlike impulse. It also is not a characteristic that remains stationary. We cannot simply download it from somewhere and be good to go. It has a learning curve. Patience is not a passive pursuit. It needs to be cultivated. How do we develop patience in the midst of a war? Let's begin by redefining what most would consider patience. Commonly, patience is defined as a calm waiting. It is that, but it is much more.

Patience requires mindfulness. I struggled with that. Maybe you can relate. As my children's destructive decisions and patterns of behavior multiplied, I found myself keeping a mental list of wrongs. Some call it "keeping score," and it is a normal communication facet in which most relationships participate off and on. It is our way of recognizing and ensuring that the terms of a relationship are being reciprocated.

After a while I noticed that my score kept cropping up every time I tried to communicate with my errant child. I had overwhelming and bad feelings at that point, and I was looking to feel justified in any way I could find. Each conversation would end with the recital of my mental list of judgments that I carried around with me every day because I had not handed them over to God.

The act of mindfulness simply means to stay in the moment and not bring other past subjects into the room with you. It is not easy to break the habit of allowing the past to rear its ugly head, but it is an act of demonstrating patience. It signifies that we have handed over all of our and our children's yesterdays and are ready to receive what God intends for today.

I often found myself needing to feel justified. I would pull up infractions from the past and add them to the present one that we were facing to gain my solid ground of intolerance. It was as if I was keeping a tally of all their wrongdoings or bad choices. I had to learn to force myself to stay in the present moment. I had to learn to actively build a tolerance for existing outside of my comfort zone.

We all tend to want to stay inside our self-prepared bubble. In other words, we want to stay in control. In my case, and maybe in yours, control had been lost. I could not stay in that place of comfortable control (have you noticed that a battlefield is *not* about comfort?). I had to nurture patience (even through mental, spiritual and physical exhaustion) to seek out new information and new routines because what I thought I knew was not helping. I was rudely demoted from queen-of-the-mountain to humble servant who was seeking and waiting on God to show me the way.

Patience in this scenario is critical because not every avenue we seek will bring forth useful information. Trial and error are parts of the journey—and that takes patience. We have to be able to get up the next day and try again even if yesterday did not bring a good result. God will always be there working through us, no matter how bad we get or how defeated our circumstances are. "And I am certain that God, who began the good work within you, will continue his work until it is finally finished on the day when Christ Jesus returns" (Philippians 1:6 NLT). God will not stop until the victory is found.

I had to absorb into every fiber of my mama's heart that accepting circumstances was part of the process. After all, you will not fight what you will not accept. Denial is not warfare. Perhaps you have been there, too. *This is surely a one-time mess up. He's going to straighten up now. This must be the last straw, the bottom of the pit. He would never consider something this crazy again.* And then he does.

It does no good to pretend that things will get better or to ignore the bad circumstances completely. We must cultivate a patience that works inside the worst of it all while still carrying the assurance that God is with us. Do not forget that God always hears our prayers no matter how big the battle becomes in the meantime. Though we may feel defeated or hopeless, God is right there working behind the scenes on our behalf. "Call to me and I will answer you and tell you great and unsearchable things you do not know" (Jeremiah 33:3).

God hears our prayers even when we do not understand. He is able to clarify what He needs us to know.

The test of resting patiently in God while battling children's behaviors, attitudes and self-destructive choices is a hard test to pass, and it is definitely not a passive action. Patience allows us to rest in God. Resting in God means that we are moving each second of every day inside of a faith that knows that at any moment God could deliver our child. As both parents and individuals, we will develop unique strategies when we are pressed and are struggling to be patient. There are, however, some that are universal to all of us.

One strategy that we must employ is to choose to stay intentional with God every day. During my Meantime Phases, I began to set up habits that I had never exercised before. Those choices kept me close to God and cultivating essential patience through the battle of unbelief and weariness. My most important habit was not to isolate in my sorrows. I made it a goal to stay connected to God, my husband, my children (yes, even though they were the cause of the pain) and trusted friends no matter what I was facing.

First, I chose a specific time to talk with God. For me, this was early in the morning before I was out of bed. I would blink my eyes and say, *God I am here, so I know You kept me alive today for a reason.* After praising and thanking Him for all I could think of, I would then share my fears, pain and hopes. Starting every day seeking His face helped me feel confident in His love, care and protection—no matter what my child had done or would do.

During this special quiet time, I would always hand my children over to God. This surrender was very similar to the story in the Bible about Abraham and his most agonizing test concerning Isaac (see Genesis 22). I would go through the motions and prayers of spiritually laying each child at the altar of God and handing them over to Him. When I surrendered their lives at the feet of God, I was handing them back to the Creator of their lives. The process allowed me to give God all my negative emotions and pain so that He could move on my behalf to save my children and mend my heart.

Throughout the day, I would cry out whenever I needed God. If I was discouraged, I would ask Him to lift me up. When I faced another setback with my child, I would cry out again to build my hope. Crying out to God seemed to be the best emergency or distress call I could make. God always heard my cries. He would answer in various ways. At times, a quiet peace would come over me from sources that could only be attributed to Him. In other instances, loving friends or family would reach out with just the right words to give me the strength to carry on. There was never a time that I cried out and entered into God's presence that I did not leave changed.

I also began to pray to God in a way similar to what Jesus demonstrated in the Lord's Prayer (see Matthew 6:9–13). I also took note that the Lord said that we were not to worry about how it sounded. It is Jesus who essentially says, "Get to the point." The verse actually says, "And when you pray, do not heap up empty phrases as the Gentiles do, for they think that they will be heard for their many words. Do not be like them, for your Father knows what you need before you ask him" (verses 7–8 ESV).

There are individuals who are touting formulas, programs and advice for getting what you want from God. Do not fall for that nonsense. God will listen as intently to you as He will anyone else on the planet. I have learned that the simple prayers of a heartbroken parent can avail much. This is your Father you are dealing with, and He knows better than you do what you need. With a God like this loving you, you can pray very simply. Here is a small sample that I have used and used.

> Our Father in heaven, reveal who You are. Set the world right, and do what is best—as above, so below. Keep us alive with three square meals. Keep us repentant before You and forgiving of others. Keep us safe from ourselves and the devil. You are in charge. You can do anything You want. You are ablaze in beauty. Yes. Yes. Yes. Amen!

As I prayed this over and over, I realized the significance of asking God to bring heaven down to earth. "Do what is best—as above, so below." Many of us are more familiar with the King James Version of Matthew 6:10: "Thy kingdom come, Thy will be done in earth, as it is in heaven." I began to believe with all of my heart that God would move on earth executing plans that were good for my child as I activated this belief in my prayers. This routine developed my patience in such a way that I still pray this prayer often in this exact manner.

Perseverance

By sheer repetition of standing in the gap for our children and showing up on the spiritual side of the war, we inherit perseverance. My definition for biblical perseverance is continuing to do good at all costs and believing that God is with us until we see our victory—because we already know that one day we will spend eternity with God. The Bible assures us that "to those who by persistence in doing good seek glory, honor and immortality, he will give eternal life" (Romans 2:7).

Perseverance defeats the devil and gives us hope to keep fighting until we meet God face to face. Our manner announces to the dark army that we will continue to strike back on behalf of our children through any opposition, difficulty or failure. Perseverance shows Satan that we are not going away. Just as God will never forsake our child, neither will we.

If you were to ask fellow Christians what their opinion is of the apostle Paul, most would agree that, besides Jesus, he could be the most influential man in history. But he did not start out that way. It was through patience and perseverance that Paul accumulated both his ministry and his reputation. Do you hear the enemy whisper? "You can never cultivate patience that transcends into perseverance. Your child is too far gone. Give up."

Paul must have felt the same way at times. He was first known as a deeply religious ruler, and then as a murderer of Christians. On his way to continue his persecution of the early Church, he went through a lightning-quick conversion to Christ on the road to Damascus. After a period of learning and waiting, he was off on the mission trail (see Acts 9).

It does not sound as though he had many tools for his journey. In fact, in the beginning few believed that Paul was truly converted. They rejected his message of the Gospel. He was beaten, whipped, stoned and imprisoned. After Mark deserted Paul and Barnabas, Barnabas also went a separate way. But Paul persevered.

Does that make him a superman? Did he have a cape that is not described in the Bible? Of course not. Paul can be counted as persevering for one single reason: When God told him to go, he kept going. We will show up for as long as we possibly can when it comes to our children, and we will be counted among those who persevere. God knew we would care for them enough to allow patience to grow as we persevered by showing up again and again.

Perspective

Finally, we need to address *perspective*. We must have an eternal lens through which we view our children's outcomes throughout the fight. The only way to see through the eyes of God perpetually and to stay eternally minded is to remain in God's Word and speak it often. The Bible reminds us that "Death and life are in the power of the tongue" (Proverbs 18:21 KJV).

We must guard against speaking any words of defeat, unbelief or hopelessness about our children. We are to talk about life and only life for our children's futures. It is hard to watch our kids reject their upbringing, choose unacceptable lifestyles or make damaging choices and yet continue to speak positively about them.

This is the point where we must realize that our parenting perspective must change. Instead of seeing the chaos and calamity, we must choose to see what we are believing God for—not denying the chaos and calamity but seeing it through God's eyes. His perspective must become ours. When we do that, we can choose to speak words of life, purpose and future both over and to our children. In doing so, we demonstrate that we know this is only a season that, with God's help, will pass. God holds His plans for their lives.

Another powerful aspect of speaking words of life to our children is that we represent how God loves and sees them. Just as God has loved each of us through good and bad, He does the same for our children, even as we continue to make the distinction between enabling bad behavior and showing love as He would.

On a daily basis, our perspective is shaped by more than God and our children's behavior. For your own sake, be careful whom you allow to verbalize thoughts about your life or those of your children. Many family members, friends, co-workers and other believers will try to share thoughts and opinions about your battle. Most people have no idea how detrimental their judgments can be for our children. When someone close to you begins to speak into your life or over your children, be prepared to stop the flow. Create a pre-determined way of gently stopping words that are not life-giving.

I would say, "Thank you so much, but I believe God is moving on our behalf." Or I would say, "Thank you so much for your concern, but I would rather not talk about it right now." The pronouncements of others may seem harmless, but when taken in context with the Bible, why risk it? Also, our challenges are such that we should surround ourselves with people who remain positive and upbeat. They should be well-versed in the Word of God. These are members of our unit in God's army.

As we build our patience, step into perseverance and take on the ability to change our perspective, we gain more and more insight and the ability to recognize when God is working behind the scenes. And during the times when we see absolutely nothing, our ever-developing patience opens the door wider and wider to the realization that God is moving even though we cannot see Him.

Even on our worst days of facing the greatest giants in the war over our children, we have power when we practice these tools. As we partner with God, actively waiting on Him, resting in Him, crying out to Him, activating heaven on earth and filtering the words of life for our children, the Meantime Phase is do-able!

PRECEPTS OF THE THREE Ps

Patience

The LORD is good to those who wait for Him, to the soul who seeks Him.

Lamentations 3:25 NKJV

But if we hope for what we do not see, we wait for it with patience.

Romans 8:25 ESV

"The LORD will fight for you; you need only to be still."

Exodus 14:14

Perseverance

So let's not get tired of doing what is good. At just the right time we will reap a harvest of blessing if we don't give up.

Galatians 6:9 NLT

For you have need of endurance, so that when you have done the will of God, you may receive what was promised.

Hebrews 10:36 NASB

Blessed is the one who perseveres under trial because, having stood the test, that person will receive the crown of life that the Lord has promised to those who love him.

James 1:12

Perspective

So we fix our eyes not on what is seen, but on what is unseen, since what is seen is temporary, but what is unseen is eternal.

2 Corinthians 4:18

For I consider that the sufferings of this present time are not worthy to be compared with the glory which shall be revealed in us.

Romans 8:18 NKJV

Jesus Christ is the same yesterday and today and forever.

Hebrews 13:8 ESV

WHAT CAN I DO TODAY?

Focus on the fact that exhibiting patience includes action. On an index card, write out your favorite verse from each of the three categories above—patience, perseverance and perspective. Make it a point to speak them aloud daily from now on. Every time you practice patience, jot it down in your journal or on the back of the card. Do this until you can see easily when your patience is at work.

A PRAYER FOR PATIENCE AND PERSPECTIVE

Father, I need Your help every day to build more patience. Lord, when it gets scary or when I find myself in the Meantime Phase, I ask for the patience, perspective and strength to persevere to hold fast to hope until I see Your plans fulfilled. I know that if I do not give up, I will receive a reward one day—most importantly, that of living with You eternally. Lord, help me to wait patiently while I hold on to the belief that on this earth healing will happen for my children. I know that You have many blessings in store for them, and I look forward to seeing them all come into fruition. I love You and praise Your holy name. You are my source and my resource. In Jesus' name, Amen.

A Different Kind of Trust

It is another new day with another sleepless night because your child did not make it home. Your stomach is upset, and your nerves are shot. Emotions are at an all-time high, and fear has overcome you. Trust with your prodigal is broken again, and you have no idea how it could ever be rebuilt. Instinctively, you know that it is time to trust God yet again. But how do you continue to do that over and over?

You may or may not have had a dad who loved you dearly. If you did, you are very blessed, and it was probably easy for you to develop an abiding trust. You never had to wonder if he would intentionally hurt you, and you could rely on the fact that your dad had your best interests at heart.

My dad was an amazing provider. He was seventeen years old when he graduated from high school and married my mom. As they raised five children, they had to work very hard. There were times that Dad worked three jobs at once to provide for us. He gave us a beautiful home, and we always had food on the table. There were not many frills, but we never felt as if we were in lack. Dad's love was demonstrated through his generous provision to our family.

Dad also always made me feel safe. When I was a teenager, our class got a new choir teacher. This teacher could not stand me. One day he decided to punish me by paddling. I called my dad before allowing the teacher to spank me. My dad got in his car immediately. He arrived at the school and told the teacher that he would never be allowed to paddle his teenage daughter. Dad went to the principal, too. I never had to be fearful again because my dad was there to rescue me from danger.

Generally, fathers take on tremendous roles in the family. They also encourage their children. My dad always made me feel that nothing was unobtainable if I put my mind to it. No matter what I dreamed, he inspired me to chase after it. Looking back, I realize that he was an entrepreneur who had experienced fulfilling dreams in his life that he felt would never be possible. Dad was always supportive. Fathers can be our number one cheerleaders against all the odds that we face.

Most importantly, fathers are to be the spiritual guides of the home. They guide us into the Word of God and take us to church. My dad never missed a service. We went Sunday morning, Sunday night and Wednesday night to church as an entire family. My dad was a greeter at the church. He was great at making everyone feel loved, as though they belonged there. Dad was always imparting and demonstrating to me how to live as a Christ-follower. His spiritual guidance and revelations were integral in helping me believe in God and understand that God loved me. If we grew up under similar circumstances, it might be fairly easy to engage in a long-lasting trust with God.

But perhaps you cannot identify with my story because of a less-than-perfect relationship with your earthly father. If so, you probably know by now that you have been deprived of an earthly template that you most likely needed in childhood. This fact can represent a challenge for how you are to trust God when you could not trust a man. Take heart. God is a greater Father than any earthly one could have been to you. Please read on, while praying to have Him help you separate the differences between human and deity. They are most assuredly not the same.

A Look at Our Heavenly Father

Even the greatest earthly fathers do not compare to the heavenly Father, but there are several similarities between them that help us understand more about who our heavenly Father is to us.

As we have seen, our earthly father works to supply us with basic provisions. He takes care of us by making sure that food is in the kitchen and that there are clothes on our backs. Our heavenly Father says that He clothes the flowers, and we are more valuable than them to Him (see Matthew 6:28–30).

One of the most touching stories in the Bible was when God caught Adam and Eve in their disobedience, and they realized they were naked. Even though God was heartbroken that they had defied His instructions, He was filled with compassion when they were embarrassed because of their nakedness. God even made them coverings so that they would come out of hiding. Genesis 3:21 says, "The LORD God made garments of skin for Adam and his wife and clothed them." He showed how much He still cared for them in the midst of their sin.

Most earthly fathers are intent on working and earning enough money to provide whatever the family needs. So does our heavenly Father. He is often called *Jehovah Jireh*, a God who is more than enough for us. God never wants us in lack. He wants to be the supplier of all the things we need.

Our earthly father teaches us how to do things, and he often instructs us in worldly things we need to learn. He also teaches us the spiritual things of life. Many times, as we follow our heavenly Father by reading His Word and praying to Him often, He, too, will give us direction and guidance. "I will instruct you and teach you in the way you should go; I will counsel you with my loving eye on you" (Psalm 32:8).

Unconditional Love Is the Difference

There also are some great differences between our earthly father and our heavenly Father. The love of our earthly father pales in comparison to our heavenly Father's love. God's love is incomprehensible and remains unconditional. Humans cannot fathom completely the love our heavenly Father has for us. God will never lie to us or be at a loss as to what is best for us. Our divine Father is infinite in wisdom and is the beginning and the end of life. There is no weakness or evil inside our heavenly Father.

Sometimes our earthly fathers make mistakes. Our heavenly Father is perfect. There is none like Him in the whole universe. He is someone we can always count on, and He will never leave us or forsake us regardless of how far we fall from His grace. We will never be alone, because we will eventually leave our earthly bodies behind and go with Him through eternity. He is the Supreme Being and is intangible.

Before we can learn to trust God, we must know who He is and what His character is. There are four main characteristics of our heavenly Father: omnipotence, omnipresence, omnibenevolence and omniscience. His omnipotence demonstrates unlimited power. His omnipresence means that He is everywhere at one time. God's characteristic of omnibenevolence shows His unlimited and perfect goodness. Finally, His omniscience declares that He knows everything there is to know.

Although our initial thoughts about who God is may have been based on what we saw in our earthly fathers, we can grow in our relationship with our heavenly Father as we get to know Him better. We can start with the truth that He will always love us and that He will have never-ending compassion for us.

Trusting God can be difficult for some. Doubt and skepticism are the most prevalent components that creep into our mind and heart and leave us in a state of distrust. As believers, those two ideas are not worth entertaining. On the day we professed Jesus as our Savior, we also acknowledged that God deserves our trust much more than humans do.

Let's dig deeper into trusting God with our children and our lives. Trusting anything when our children are in hell is brutally difficult. It is far easier to manage our emotions if we simply decide that we will irrevocably trust God no matter what happens. It is our first act in choosing God's ways, plans, protection and provision—even when facing fear and hopelessness. The best way to overcome distrust and anxiety is to know that God can be trusted with everything, whether we fully comprehend our circumstances or not.

It is magnificently comforting to know that, on behalf of our children, there is nothing—no sin, shameful act or addiction—that can separate them from God's love. It truly encompasses more than any of us can fathom. God sees the good, bad and ugly, and He still chooses to love our children extravagantly. This happens even while the great deceiver, Satan, tries everything in his power to separate them from Him and from us.

The devil also attempts to deliver the message to us that they are too far gone, even for God's expansive love and care to bring them back. He will frequently try to fill us with fear that our children will never be healed or delivered. The demons on earth keep us wrapped up in negative emotions in an effort to disconnect us from God and His promises. The word *trust* is defined as "an assured reliance on the character, ability, strength, or truth of someone or something."[1] We can use this description to explore God further.

Firm belief requires that we are convinced that God is real. It is vital that we ask ourselves, "Do I believe that God is real, alive and all powerful today?" No one can answer this question for us. If we are entertaining even the slightest bit of doubt, then we must start building our belief that God is the Creator of all. Once we confirm in our heart, mind, soul and spirit that He is the one true God, our trust strengthens.

The word *reliable* is defined as "consistently good in quality or performance; able to be trusted."[2] We must know that God is good and that He will act on our behalf. The Bible tells us that only God is good (see Luke 18:19). What does this mean? It is one of the many descriptions of who God is, and He shows this in many ways. God presents us with the gift of mercy, provides for us in more ways than we can recognize, leads us through the battles with our children and watches over all of us. When we absorb and receive His goodness, we can expect only good outcomes in both our lives and those of our children. His amazing goodness only adds fuel to our trust in Him.

Before we can move on to the concept of truth, we must address two asides to ascertain what truth looks like. Humans tend to confuse truth with opinions and judgments. Opinions are views that are not necessarily based on facts. In many instances, our opinions are based on experiences. A judgment is very different in that it is formed. It is a decision that we have carefully weighed and have come to a conclusion about. Usually, a judgment is a statement that is firm.

Both opinions and judgments can be flawed. I was raised in the South around many farms. Most were stocked with horses, chickens and cows. I loved seeing the cows. I was particularly fond of how they sought a reprieve from the summer heat by lying in the shade of the nearest tree. My brother and sisters knew how excited I became when we passed a herd in a field. Every time we saw brown, white and black cows in one place, my siblings always took time to "educate" me. They told me that chocolate milk was made from black cows. For many of my childhood years, I made the judgment that black cows produced chocolate milk. Although I was told this about cows for years, it was not true.

Truth is not an opinion or a judgment; the truth is decided by God. The world is full of lies, but God's spiritual world is all based on truth. When we are faced with questions about what to do or how to live as God desires, we must have faith that the Word of God is the only way to measure truth. When we need answers, the correct instructions are often found in the written Word of God. Trusting that the Bible is the only truth is the way to live according to God's will and plans.

The word *ability* is the next term to understand as we build our trust with God. It is massively different from human ability. If trusting in God was based purely on human endeavor, we would always be missing key components. God's ability relates to doing something on our behalf, including receiving help with growing our trust. It is only with God that we accomplish anything. Our narrow ideas of His abilities are still enough to increase our trust in what He is capable of.

The last word used in describing trust is *strength*. Envision the act of weight lifting. As the body becomes stronger, we increase the resistance. Strength training is an excellent analogy to use for increasing our trust in God. It often takes going through adversity successfully to build our trust muscles with God. Our muscles relax as the winds of our storm calm, but they will have strengthened a bit more so that they are stronger for the next storm. Each time we partner with Him, the cycle repeats itself. The goal is not to stop working in this area until our trust in Him has become second nature.

I define God's endless capacity moving through my life as *grace*. The mountain I need to climb or the test I need to pass can only be completed with what He endows for the journey. I cannot navigate by myself through this life that is full of hurts. Grace can be found every day when I realize that God is moving through me to obtain a good outcome.

A recognition of the presence of His grace did not come to me until later in life. I was almost 38 when I discovered fully what grace meant. Grace is not a religious word, but it is a word that transformed my relationship with God. I knew about God and went to church all my life, but I had never comprehended His amazing grace. In simple terms, I did not see that God loved me regardless of how many sins I committed yesterday, today or tomorrow. It was His grace through the blood of Jesus on a cross that covered everything I would ever do.

Embrace Grace

Maybe you are like me, and grace is merely a word. Perhaps it has not yet been an experience that you and God have intimately shared. When I received this forgiveness and grace that covered all my life and the life I had yet to live, it changed everything. I no longer looked at God from afar. I no longer saw God as a rule keeper who was tallying all my sins. I only saw God's amazing grace flowing out of His Son's death on a cross.

If we underestimate the value of Jesus' death on a cross, we are bound to religion. Religious mindsets can be another snare of the enemy. Satan knows that we will never be close to God if we live in sin and self-condemnation. Satan's greatest wish is that we never know God intimately and never have a deep personal relationship with the Creator of the universe. When we receive God's grace that was freely given to us through the sacrifice of His only Son, then we can begin to trust Him with our life as well our children's.

Even knowing all the above, I am aware that trust is one of the most difficult facets to navigate when our children are sinking. Yet when we think and pray it through, we quickly come to the conclusion that we must anchor our hope on something both firm and eternal. We have no other options than to believe that the Maker of the whole world and the Father of all will work out His promises and words in our children's lives.

When the fires of hell are heating up and we are facing imminent loss, God is the only One we can trust to quench the fire and open the door to a rescue. No human could do that for us. Trusting God does not necessarily prevent battles with the enemy over our children, but our faith keeps us hoping that God can step in and change everything at any given time. Trust keeps us confident and fighting. God deserves our trust.

TAKING THE TRUST TEST

Keeping in mind that this is about honesty and not about right or wrong, rate yourself on these trust statements using the following scale: Absolutely = 10, Somewhere In Between = 9–2, Never = 1

- ▶ I trust God enough to seek Him out daily.
  Rate: ___

- ▶ I trust what is written in the Bible, and I am willing to apply those truths to my life.
  Rate: ___

- ▶ I trust that all of God's promises are meant for every member of my family.
  Rate: ___

- ▶ I trust that God will rescue my children.
  Rate: ___

- ▶ I trust that God is working behind the scenes all the time.
  Rate: ___

- ▶ I trust God more than I trust any human being.
  Rate: ___

WHAT CAN I DO TODAY?

Few of us have a rating of ten on every trust statement. We can start the habit of developing trust in God by writing the following on an index card and reciting it at every opportunity:

> Trust in the LORD with all your heart and lean not on your own understanding; in all your ways submit to him, and he will make your paths straight.
>
> Proverbs 3:5–6

PRAYER FOR TRUST

Father, I am trying hard to learn to trust You more, especially in the storms of life. Help me to build my trust as I move together through Your Word and Your promises for myself and my family. Show me how to anchor myself in You. I need You every day, and I depend on You to help me navigate the ongoing spiritual war in my life. I commit to trusting You with all that I have and all that I am. In Jesus' name, Amen.

The Significance of Surrender

Practically speaking, what does surrender look like? We typically begin by aligning our lives and actions within spiritual parameters and allowing God to guide us. We must choose to go to God first and not make our decisions based off of what pops into our heads on impulse. When we are weak and discouraged, it is hard for us to see clearly or to make great decisions. The best answer is to default to God's will.

Part of learning to surrender the control of our life to Him is handing Him the ability to take the lead in every area of our life. This level of surrender ensures that God is in control. Although fights may still occur with our children, we know that God will help us. God will give us the words to speak, and He will guide us into the next right step.

Most importantly, when the storms are volatile and scary, we know that God essentially controls the outcome. An airplane flight is an excellent example of surrender. We buy our ticket, board the plane, trust the pilot and expect to land at the chosen destination. Think about everything we do *not* know or understand in the process. Surrender to God is buying His salvation plan, trusting Him to bring victory to the war over the enemy and then finally living eternally with Him in heaven.

There was a time in Kaylee's life when it looked as if she would die. She had been rushed from college to the hospital in our hometown. She could not lift her head and was not able to function. She was hospitalized for days as the doctors ran tests. Many of them, such as a spinal tap, were very invasive. They gave her medicines, but she was not getting well. Basically, after weeks in the hospital, the doctors agreed that it would be best to send her home. They said they had done all they could do for her medically.

During this horrible battle as the devil was trying to kill my daughter through illness, I was reminded of a story in the Bible with Abraham and Isaac. Abraham was a chosen man of God. He was the father of faith, and we are all his descendants. One day God tested Abraham's faith (see Genesis 22). God asked Abraham to lay his son, Isaac, on the altar to sacrifice him.

Abraham gathered all of the material he needed. As he and Isaac walked up the mountain to prepare the altar, Isaac asked, "What are we going to sacrifice to God?" Abraham laid his son down on the altar, tied him down and prepared to cut him with a knife. At that moment, an angel appeared to Abraham. "'Don't lay a hand on the boy!' the angel said. 'Do not hurt him in any way, for now I know that you truly fear God'" (Genesis 22:12 NLT). When our children are hurting, whether it is from their own choices or not, we must surrender them to God in an altar-like place.

After I had spent days by Kaylee's bedside in the hospital as she suffered, I was persuaded to go home and shower. When I drove up to my driveway and parked, I felt led to go outside to our pool. Beside the water, I fell to my knees. I cried out to God, and I begged God to relieve Kaylee of her pain. Then I mentally laid Kaylee down at the feet of God on an altar similar to Abraham's.

In my spirit and soul, I said to God, *Here is Kaylee on the altar. I would rather You take her life and heal her in heaven than have her suffer.* I surrendered Kaylee's physical body at the altar of God. I would still rather lose her here on earth and have her be free of sickness in the loving Father's arms than to know that she is suffering.

Surrendering in today's world almost always has a negative connotation. Surrendering to God is yielding to Him. To demonstrate this, let's look at a traffic light. The red light means stop. The green light means go. The yellow lights mean yield, caution and proceed with care. Surrendering is consulting with God regularly. *What do I do next, and is it safe?* It is looking to God for our best care. Surrendering to God is where we find the power to trust Him with our children. We must yield to God, giving Him the control, so that He can show us our next move to win our battles.

There are a few concepts to unpack when it comes to the notion of surrendering our children to God. First, we must tackle its opposite: control. By exploring and possibly discovering the truths on surrender and control, we can better manage the outcome of taking back our child from the devil.

Control

As parents, we tend to believe (either consciously, subconsciously or both) that we are able to control our family. And perhaps for large portions of time, we have good reason to think so. When our children are smaller, they typically obey our rules. Why would we not believe those behaviors would continue? There is a saying that the smaller the child, the smaller the problems. This means that a scraped knee or small issues are easily healed. But the problems that can show up with bigger kids, like a citation for driving under the influence (DUI) or other life-altering problems, are not so easily resolved. As our adorable little tykes grow up to be disobedient teens and young adults, we experience the complex realization that we are no longer controlling many portions of their lives.

When we begin to recognize that our grip is loosening, we often feel forced to manipulate our children in ways that are meant to have them act or behave better. The more our children act up or disobey, the more we try to manage and control their actions and bad decisions. This merry-go-round parenting can spiral into an endless stream of push and be pushed. It takes a lot of trial and error to figure out that we have become much like the kitten who perpetually chases its tail.

As all three of my children spiraled into the darkness of hell, the first thing I tried to do was regain control over them. I would punish wrong choices. I put boundaries on activities and social schedules. I tried everything I could think of to fashion their lives in such a way as to provide a better outcome for their behaviors. I only succeeded in failing my children and myself. I was not allowing God to control the situation or allowing Him to move through their wrong choices.

Instead of being a mom who was certain that God had things handled, I looked like a mean tyrant. As a result, my children's disdain for me only got worse, which made them more defiant than ever. In turn, I felt as though I was responsible for their bad choices since I had been making wrong choices, too. We were all losing the battle!

The remedy for my miserable merry-go-round parenting cycle started when I realized that I had never been in control in the first place. My manipulation could never produce anything other than losing a battle. I had to give to God any perceived control that I thought I had over my children; I had to surrender them. In simple terms, *surrender* means "to give oneself up into the power of another."[1] This was yet another pivotal point in the war for my children against evil. If I truly believed that God had a plan for my children, then I would never be in control of their choices. I was only a parent to guide and protect them as best I could. As adults, we frequently reach out to God and call Him Father. It had not occurred to me that He was their actual parent in ways that I was not able to be.

When we hear the word *surrender*, we often think of it with a negative connotation. The word brings on feelings of loss, misery and even death. These are certainly things that we do not voluntarily sign up to participate in. The good news is that surrender to God can be easy. The type of surrender we are discussing is the act of handing everything over to Him.

When we look at this in the appropriate spiritual hierarchy format, God is the Father of all. We, as earthly parents, are symbolically handing our child back to God to affirm this truth. We are relinquishing control over our own lives and surrendering our children's lives to acknowledge God's supreme authority. In doing so, we open ourselves to His help in turning things around.

Our double surrender signifies that we have joined in partnership with Him and no longer consider ourselves the leader. We are willing soldiers in God's army for the sake of our children. We open the door to allow other people and resources that He provides into the situation. Partnering with God means unlimited help is coming in ways we are not capable of imagining.

Unlike the prevailing mindset that when someone surrenders, they lose, when we surrender to God, we receive three of the greatest and most needed blessings: peace, confidence and hope.

Peace

Once we know that God is present and He is active in our children's lives, a measure of spiritual peace is available—even if the behavior of our child has not changed. We can dwell in the comfort that God is right there with us and sees all that we see. We are not alone in facing the challenges with our children. A new level of response to our children exists when they are disobedient. It is possible for anger to recede into the background and have God's peace overflow in our hearts. As we interact with our prodigals, our emotions can move aside so that we can truly hear them and learn what is driving them and their current behavior and choices. This information can be vital to our prayer life and meditation times with God.

Confidence

The second blessing found in surrender is confidence. As our children make self-destructive choices, we start to lose faith in ourselves and our parenting skills. We often find ourselves carrying the added burden of extremely low self-esteem. God never intended anyone to live outside of his or her identity through Him. This does not change based on what our children are doing. Our spirit can be brought to new levels as we partner with Him concerning our children. Even when the worst demonic battle is seemingly won over our child, we can still find confidence and courage in the truth. Do not hesitate to repeat what you believe aloud for all the demons of the dark army to hear. In fact, you can practice right now by proclaiming, "God has got my prodigal child! No weapon will succeed against him/her!" Increased confidence brings on additional boldness and the strength to carry on, no matter how hard the fighting gets.

Hope

The third blessing we will find in surrender is the one that will equip us for battle after battle with our prodigal. This special blessing is hope. There are many components to hope, but one that is often overlooked is that hope can be grown and expanded. Hope is an attribute that we would do well to cultivate and develop consistently. The act of surrendering puts us on fertile soil for cultivating hope. It could be called the fuel that keeps us fighting.

F.O.C.U.S.

I rely on an acronym that helps me to build hope: F. O. C. U. S. It might be advantageous to provide a definition. I define it as the process of allowing our eyes to adapt to the prevailing level of light to be able to see clearly. When we see victory in our future clearly, then our hope has reached the level of unlimited! Let's look at the five facets of F. O. C. U. S.

The F reminds us to *focus on the spiritual*. We must ask ourselves a few questions. What are we focusing on? What are we highlighting in our thoughts and mind every day?

Now is the time to shift the majority of our thinking to an eternal lens. Let's blur out the temporary and begin to see our environment through the lens of God.

When we can see that God is more significant than what we face and that He sees the end of our story in victory, our entire attitude changes. We can resist going through the mechanics of life in the doldrums and, instead, embrace each moment in expectation. Instead of staying in a negative thought process that sounds something like, "My child will never find healing," focus on what God can do. The short answer is: anything!

He is already working behind the scenes to show you the way to a breakthrough. When we think about the optimistic promises of God, especially concerning our children, we are given a sustainable measure of hope to carry us through the war. As long as we focus primarily on the spiritual side of the battle, we are reassured that victory is coming.

This leads us to the O in our acronym, which represents *opting out of negative activity*. During the worst of times, we find it necessary to evaluate our ongoing activities in three specific areas. Distractions are a major weapon of the enemy. There is absolutely nothing wrong with social media, books, podcasts or television. It is only when we become ensconced for huge amounts of time in an effort to numb ourselves to life that they can be defined as a danger to our mission to save our children.

There are three distinct questions we should ask ourselves in the event we suspect we are participating in escapism of any sort.

- Is this activity taking up valuable time that could be spent in pursuit of my partnership with God for the sake of my children?

- Am I scrolling through social media or buying books to read about the life I dream of instead of facing the one I currently have?
- Does the content I watch serve to educate or inspire me, or does it frequently leave me feeling more burdened than before?

Put bluntly, we need to get rid of as many negative distractions as possible. Is the news depressing to you? If so, why watch? There are news apps for our phones that give us the bare headlines and weather. And, of course, families and children look perfect on social media and in fictional stories. Reality does not make our family a failure.

The war is not yet over, and we have not yet seen the amazing things God has in store for our family. Comparison will only serve to permanently destroy our days and remove any opportunity we would have had to take a positive stand for our children. Our goal is to keep depositing the positive in our lives and opting out of the negative.

C represents *considering the core* of our lives. The most valuable things in our lives are our family and friends. We should examine whether or not we are giving these things the time they deserve. Are we being intentional about building and keeping these relationships nurtured and fed? The special people we have in our lives are fundamental to hope. So often, our attention goes to the squeakiest wheel.

When our children are actively in destructive behavior, our eyes are usually on them. It is vital that we refrain from focusing only on what is wrong. We should also look around to find the people who have been supportive and loving and continue nurturing those relationships. These are the people who have chosen to make the journey with us, and there will be times when we desperately need them. We must not neglect them.

The letter U stands for *understanding our true identity*. As we learned earlier, our identity must be anchored in Christ. In our hearts, we need to know that we were hand-knit in our mother's womb by God. God created us. He designed us. He is there for us. He knows all our weaknesses, habits and character flaws. When we realize that God is not surprised, even by our reactions and failures, we begin to live differently with no more self-condemnation or self-doubt.

Our final letter in the acronym is S. It stands for *sustained power*. We often need a reminder that we have a sustaining, eternally supportive power that allows us to face whatever challenges life throws at us. By focusing on the eternal, by opting out of negative activity, by considering our core, by understanding our true identity and by embracing the sustained power to live, we will stir up our foundation of hope. As we war for our children, the *only* place we want to surrender is with God.

In the military sense, that means ceasing our own resistance to an enemy or opponent and submitting to our authority. We surrender our battle to the darkness by submitting our children to the supreme authority—God. It is a huge decision. As the battles rage and we get weary of conflict with our wayward child, we win the battle by surrendering it all to God.

After I surrendered my daughter to God, she recovered fully. She was healed supernaturally with many prayers and petitions. We were so blessed to have experienced God's supernatural goodness, and this altar-like experience became a practice for surrendering all three of my children many times in their hellish years. I would often lay them down at the feet of God, place them on an altar and surrender them to God's complete authority, control and power.

As we battle for our children, surrender is a strategic, winning and defensive action. We hand God full ownership of our prodigal child, and we relinquish control over him or her. We submit to God's authority, and we trust in Him for the victorious outcome. The merry-go-round parenting is extinguished, and we quit manipulating our children. We lay our troubled children at God's feet, handing over everything to Him.

LET'S F.O.C.U.S.

Focus on the spiritual
Opt out of negative activity
Consider our core
Understand our true identity
Sustained power

WHAT CAN I DO TODAY?

The act of surrendering often means uncomfortable admissions. Remember that God already knows what you are meant to surrender. He is merely waiting for you to partner with Him. Write the following on an index card as a reminder to surrender everything daily.

> So humble yourselves before God. Resist the devil, and he will flee from you.
>
> James 4:7 NLT

Today I need to surrender:

1.

2.

3.

4.

5.

PRAYER OF SURRENDER

Father, I am so thankful that You are willing to share my burdens. Help me to surrender all that I am to You. I surrender my thoughts, words and deeds. I accept any correction or instruction You supply. Most importantly, I hand over the most precious items of my life to You. I acknowledge that my children belonged to You first, and I surrender them back to You in full assurance that You will bring them back from the enemy. No weapon has been formed that You have not foreseen and cannot overcome. In Jesus' name, Amen.

10

Initial Responses

A certain amount of defying the wishes and authority of parents is a natural part of growing up. If we take a walk down memory lane, we will recall more than one incident when we exhibited the same behavior toward our parents. Maybe it started when we refused to eat our peas and quietly stuffed them inside our napkins. Or perhaps there came a day during school when we decided not to turn in required homework and see what happened. Then, there might have been those times when some of us dared to skip school with our friends, hoping against hope that our parents would not be notified, but willing to take the heat even if they were.

These all represent episodes related to figuring out who we are, expressing ourselves or trying to establish a bit of independence. For most of us, the ensuing punishment was enough to teach us that most rebellious acts were not worth the effort.

What is not considered normal—or even acceptable—is the angry, argumentative, spiteful or rebellious behaviors we could have chosen to respond with when we eventually got caught. It is this inappropriate behavior that contributes to a downward spiral in the communication between parent and child. As these conflicts mount, they also contribute to the sheer exhaustion of parenting.

The Bible is replete with Scripture verses concerning our children. There are some verses that are addressed directly to the child, including advising a son to "hear the instruction of your father, and do not forsake the law of your mother; for they will be a graceful ornament on your head, and chains about your neck" (Proverbs 1:8–9 NKJV). Obviously, the wayward child does not feel that way or agree with the Scripture passage, but that does not detract from the further implications inside the verse. As parents, it suggests that we are to deliver instruction and boundaries regardless of how our children might feel about it.

The pressure today from society is that we become our children's best friends; however, we cannot be both parents and friends. There is a healthy balance between being a good parent to our child and being a good friend to them. The goal is to be close to our children—for sure like a friend—but stay inside the role of parent. We must be always an authority. We need to be able to discipline and have the last word on things. The level of closeness and being a friend to our child will change with each season and age, but we always need to establish that we are, in fact, the parent first and foremost.

As we have discussed previously, trying to figure out which way to go in choosing various types of parental directives can be quite confusing. But there are a few basics we can stand by as we listen to God for further advice. Let's look at them now.

Necessities versus Privileges

It is doubtful that our recalcitrant children are able to make any distinction between necessities and privileges. Most kids nowadays consider devices a maintenance item and not something they can actually draw a breath without. It is helpful that we make a list of all the ancillary luxuries we have supplied to our children. We can then set up a system by which the privileges of using said items can be removed for a period if our children refuse to comply with house rules or if they exhibit other forms of defiance and disrespect. The object of establishing the system is not to promote punishment, but rather to gain cooperation within household guidelines. The common family rules are meant to apply to every single member without exclusion. It is not okay to stretch and bend the rules to avoid facing inevitable confrontations.

Tone of Conversation

Another basic and practical habit that can occur immediately is the cessation of nagging, repeating instructions or screaming. Nagging is a cultivated habit, which means we can work on ceasing the behavior. The easiest way to find out if we are habitual naggers is to ask those closest to us. If the answer is yes, then it is time to really listen to our words as they flow from our mouth.

Think about how you might respond to hearing the same phrases over and over—no matter what is being said. How long would it take before you no longer felt any obligation to give the pronouncement any heed? If you repeatedly heard, "I promise! You're going to receive a million dollars soon," after a while, would you believe it? The same is true of our children. Sooner or later, repeated phrases start going in one ear and out the other almost as quickly as they are heard.

The act of screaming often brings forth an emotional response that has nothing to do with the words being spoken. In fact, many experts refer to yelling at someone as a form of verbal or emotional abuse—or both.[1] It is also interesting to note that yelling threats that are overheard by others could be considered assault. All three of these communication habits only serve, in the end, to lessen the impact of our authority.[2]

It is healthier for both sides if parents give directions one time, making sure they are clearly understood. After that, one warning about potential consequences is sufficient. When our boss walks into the office and gives directions, we tend to listen to them and not ignore them. The concept is the same here. Parents are the "co-bosses" of the household. The Bible tells us, "Start children off on the way they should go, and even when they are old they will not turn from it" (Proverbs 22:6). Clearly, God intends for us to be the parent. Yes, God is the ultimate parent of our child, but He instructs us to share His love and instructions with our children so that they will always come back no matter how far away they may wander.

Follow Through

If we are still ignored after the steps above, we will need to follow through with consequences. This, of course, is the least enjoyable part of the transaction. Before issuing instructions and consequences, we must think through what an appropriate punishment for each type of behavior would be. Be careful not to overdo or underdo. We want our children to be corrected, but not be completely imprisoned for smaller incidents. Let the punishment equal the offense.

Most importantly, we must never threaten a consequence we are not willing to enforce. If we do not follow through with enforcement, we lessen the impact of our authority. It is often the result of allowing our emotions to lead the way in a situation rather than our plan. We should avoid falling into the trap of becoming as rude or disrespectful as our children have been. Our role is to model the behavior we would prefer them to exhibit.

Allowing Consequences

We should also avoid taking up for our children when they have broken certain societal rules. If Sam receives detention at school because he failed to turn in three assignments, it does no good to make excuses for him. In fact, if we rush to defend him, it could teach him that Mom thinks it is okay for him to bend or break school rules. If Martha is called into the principal's office for calling her teacher a vulgar name, the parent must agree with school authorities that her behavior is unacceptable. We can think in terms of how we prefer our children to act when they graduate into adulthood. What we support now is how they will act later.

It is tempting to respond as if the behavior our child has demonstrated is a direct reflection of who we are as parents. The majority of the time that is simply not the case. At a certain point, it is time to stop owning what our children do. There is no end to the myriad of choices our children can make even though they absolutely know we would not support them. If they are not asking if it is okay, then it is safe to assume they have put on the rebellion hat and are proceeding at will.

Give Praise When Due

On the flip side, we need to readily compliment or thank our children for the good choices they make. There is huge value in making our children aware that we are paying attention to all of their behavior—not just the negative. It might prove challenging, especially in the beginning of a battle, but we should do our best to ensure our children hear praise more often than they do criticism. Here are a few suggestions:

"Thanks so much for cleaning your room without my asking."

"I've noticed how respectful you've been toward me in the last few days. Thank you."

"Thanks for putting your dishes in the sink."

"I appreciate that you brought in the garbage cans."

"I see how hard you are working to bring your grades up. Good job!"

There is no better gift to bestow on our children than letting them know we have noticed their appropriate actions. Try to put yourself in their shoes and remember what you wanted to hear most from your parents. Do not discount that you were once a child who was susceptible to mood swings, insecurities and a need for independence. Not every behavior is coming from enemy control. Some things must fall under the onus of growing up. When you establish a system that is related to household rules and ensuing consequences, you can manage the easier stuff.

Even though our children may protest otherwise, they often may not know how to go about getting out of bad situations. Consequently, it might be possible to lend a hand with problem solving along the way. If our children are open and communicating, we can listen to their dilemmas and ask what ideas they have come up with to solve the issue. If their ideas sound feasible, we can encourage them to step forward into action. If not, we can steer the conversation to a place where they can recognize how the perceived solution might lead to something worse. Sometimes, just asking what a child would do differently if they had the opportunity can help the discussion. Here are three concepts to keep in front of our children when we communicate:

First, strive to make sure that no matter how creative their solutions seem to be, they remain realistic. Many times, our kids would rather speak in flights of fantasy than face the ultimate truths in front of them.

Second, help them assemble a list of options to consider concerning a given challenge. This process encourages them to think through various avenues to step out of a situation.

Third, help them understand that decisions result in consequences. Sometimes, we have to make hard decisions. We must be ever so careful to try to make sure our child realizes she is taking an active part in working through her problems.

In the extremity, we may face a child who is intent on leaving us completely out of all decision-making processes—period. If this is the case, it may be time to pick our battles. If our children are defiant in several ways, we may have to try our new approaches with only one facet of behavior at a time. It can be very easy to overwhelm a child who has turned his life into disaster and is trying to find a way out. At all costs, we need to avoid power struggles, as they only serve to rile emotions in our child and undermine our authority. We may have to decide which conflicts are not worth our time and energy.

We should concentrate on those battles that pose a danger to our child in a very real way. Dress codes have no potential to kill our children, but driving while drunk certainly does. Physical violence to a sibling or bullying classmates should also set off a warning. Regardless of how our children might react, these are topics we cannot afford to back down on.

Always, always go to God first. After abiding in Him, we should sit down and create a plan of action that includes what we intend to communicate as well as what restrictions or punishments we intend to deliver. By preparing in advance, we can avoid jumping on the emotion wagon with our child. Our goal should be to state clearly what our child's offense is, why it has to stop, what dangers it presents and what we intend to do to make sure it does not happen again. One of your greatest challenges in heated moments—even with older children—will be to remember that you are the adult.

The core of many confrontations with our children centers on respect. Respect for another human happens when we are willing to humble ourselves in honesty and when we can be transparent about our behavior. In the heat of the battle, we often lose track of both our words and how they sound. For that reason, we can take our unconscious verbal behavior before the Lord and ask Him to help us to model what is appropriate.

Respect for an individual goes beyond saying "yes ma'am" or "no sir." When we ask our children to communicate in such a way, it is more a response of compliance. There is absolutely nothing wrong with compliant behavior. We all participate in a certain amount of it every day. We can share a measure of respect for our children if we apply compliance in return by using kind and friendly mannerisms. We must ask ourselves how often we are using words like *thank you*, *please* or *I appreciate that*. Very often we show children how to respect by respecting them.

Parenting is one of the hardest jobs in the world, and we all make mistakes. For some reason, we tend to feel that we need not acknowledge this to our children. A parent is not some superhero in a cape. We are mere humans who are doing our best and who are not perfect. It is okay for our children to know that.

And there is nothing wrong with apologizing to a child. In fact, there are a few benefits. Apologies from parents show honesty and courage. As most of us know, our prodigals do not find "I'm sorry" an easy thing to say. We, as parents, can pave the way by going first. The act of apologizing also demonstrates that it is okay to make mistakes and that they can begin to be rectified by acknowledging them.

One of the most common situations in which we find ourselves in need of apologizing is when we verbally blow up. We do not accept it when our children do it, and it is not acceptable for us, either. We can be embroiled in a confrontation in perfect parental mode, and then one phrase uttered by our child can cause us to blow the roof off our emotions. When that happens, we verbally spew in ways we should not. We are suddenly ensconced in a screaming match that is going nowhere.

At this point, the first rule of stepping up to apologize is to take a deep breath, remember who we are and calm ourselves. When words are expressed in anger and loud volume, they are unlikely to be heard. They do nothing more than set off explosive reactions in our children. In those moments, it is acceptable (and sometimes required) that we lovingly say, "I can't talk about this right now. I need to step away for a bit." This gives us the opportunity to go to God and let Him help to bring peace back into our hearts.

When we apologize, we need to keep the focus on ourselves and our own words. After all, it is what we are responsible for. We should not say things such as, "I didn't mean to go off on you like that, but you got me started when you said I was an old nag." Adding the word *but* to an apology negates the entire process, because it transfers blame to the child. We must have the courage to own our words free and clear of what anyone else has spoken.

We have control of our mouth. There is no need to define the entire confrontation when our child was there during it. It is fine to mention if there are unexplained circumstances, such as having had a bad night of sleep the night before or having had a bad day, but only if we make it plain that those circumstances do not excuse our behavior. None of us want to explode on our children, but it happens. It is a huge measure of respect if we can stand up afterward and apologize.

There is one final component of communication we should be aware of while attempting to talk to our children. We can all admit this one can really push our buttons: the silent treatment. It is often the primary weapon of choice that our children use to attempt a variety of things. The silent treatment is a fairly successful technique children use to get parents to leave them alone.

Giving them space is okay. It may be that the child is not able to formulate any type of acceptable answer in the moment. In most circumstances, they are dealing with shame or guilt. It is possible they are struggling to find some explanation that will at least partly justify their behavior.

Nonverbal interaction freezes us out. Simply put, we have nowhere to go in the absence of conversation. Its baser implication says, "I'm not giving you the satisfaction of including you in my life." As adults, we have most likely taken part in random acts of passive aggression like this. While it may not be clear where our child is coming from or what the motivation is behind the silent treatment, we will find it helpful to set boundaries for ourselves in dealing with it.

First, we can make it clear that we are fully aware of the attempt to avoid communication, but we can let them know that it does not solve anything. "I see that you believe that if you don't talk about this something will get better between us, but that is not true." Next, we can apply a particular motivation to persuade our child to talk. "Until we talk this through, you'll have to forego your cell phone. Once we sit down and have a conversation, you'll get it back." Then, doing our level best to remember that this tension is about our child and that we should not take it personally, we should go on about our business and let him or her sort through the decision-making process. Earlier we talked about the adverse effects of our nagging. It is not time to nag during the silent treatment. This will only shift power to our child.

It is not our responsibility to plead and beg our children to speak to us. Our job is always to be open and available and to listen well when they decide to engage (not berating them about the silence). That does not mean we stop speaking to our child while a difficult situation is in the air. We can and should continue to do our best to include them in normal family communication, such as that around the dinner table. This is not about anger; it is about compliance. And it is not about getting even. Do not succumb to the temptation of saying something like, "Well, I'll show him."

Our initial responses during confrontation often set the pace for the rest of the interaction. By thinking through our possibilities and reining in our emotions, we will have a better chance of achieving the goals of communicating with our children. And we will do so in a healthy way for everyone involved.

PARENTAL RESPONSES

A gentle answer turns away wrath, but a harsh word stirs up anger.

Proverbs 15:1

Be kind to one another, tenderhearted, forgiving one another, as God in Christ forgave you.

Ephesians 4:32 ESV

Do everything without complaining and arguing.

Philippians 2:14 NLT

So then, my beloved brethren, let every man be swift to hear, slow to speak, slow to wrath.

James 1:19 NKJV

WHAT CAN I DO TODAY?

Think about how your child belongs to the Lord. Write the following on an index card, add it to the others you have created and recite it at every opportunity:

Fathers [and mothers], do not provoke your children to anger, but bring them up in the discipline and instruction of the Lord.

Ephesians 6:4 ESV

PRAYER ON PARENTING

Father, thank You so much for blessing me with a child! I consider it a blessing and a gift. Even though my child and I are going through tough times, I know that You are in the battle beside me. I know You love my child even more than I do. I will do my best to raise him/her in the ways You have shown me through Your Word and instruction. Help me to respond to each situation in a way that glorifies You. In Jesus' name, Amen.

Embracing New Behaviors

When we continually battle our teens and adult children, our lives can change. It is entirely possible that we lose sight of what our old "normal" used to look like. What was it we used to do on idle Sunday afternoons? When was the last time we enjoyed reading a good book? The status of normal is different from one individual to another, but it does still exist. We can enhance our physical, mental and spiritual well-being by retaining as many supportive activities as we can.

When we are in the midst of warfare for our children, the first step in self-preservation is acknowledging that, to a degree, there are times we must separate emotionally and physically from our wayward children. We discussed in the previous chapter how unwise it is to continue to treat them as if their behavior is okay. We cannot ignore the painful facts any longer, and we must approach the issues we have with our children in ways that negate unhealthy action on our part. No matter what those approaches are, our efforts inevitably have the capacity to exhaust us as parents. Here are some necessary steps I took to help me retrieve my health and strength. I believe you will find them helpful as well.

Me/Us Care

Part of our defense within this spiritual war is doing all that we can to retain some semblance of normalcy in our lives. We can counter the devil by proactively performing adequate self-care, or what I like to call it: Me Care (or Us Care when it comes to our marriage). Me Care is doing the things that make us feel better.

What could Me Care look like? It could be a combination of a myriad of activities. When attempting to decide on what a Me Care moment might look like, we can start by asking a question: What could I do to make myself feel better right this second? The activities in this category are typically what we believe we do not have time for, or guilty pleasures. These are the things that a parent who is dealing with a distraught child seemingly should not entertain. Nothing could be further from the truth. It is when we are under extreme stress that we should spend extra time and effort on Me Care whenever possible.

There are so many fun, peaceful and relaxing things to consider. We can relax and let go by soaking in a hot tub with therapeutic bath salts added. We can also exercise. When we exercise, there is a natural release of endorphins that help to improve our mood and cause us to feel emotionally lighter. An added benefit of exercise is that it may create a more peaceful slumber.

We may want to get lost in the latest best seller. Reading allows our mind to escape and travel through our imagination to vastly different locations and circumstances. Those who love to cook can delve into favorite comfort foods to enjoy and share with others, or we can try out that new recipe we have been meaning to tackle. We can watch television or go to the movies. All of these examples serve to take our children away from the center of our attention for a while.

We can also find encouragement by being in the company of others. We can arrange to meet a friend for dinner or coffee to fellowship and visit with them about any topic other than children. Social Me Care can nourish and nurture the mind, body, soul and spirit of those of us who are more relational in nature. It allows us to focus on what is going on in the world beyond the four walls of our home.

Another place we can begin to invest in ourselves is within the pursuit of various hobbies. This is where we are free to mix our passions and sense of exploration with creativity. There are all types of hobbies to check out. Again, for the cooks, trying out classes that teach how to create foreign cuisine dishes or experimenting with new spices and techniques could be quite enjoyable. For those who love spending time outside, gardening and landscaping are options. Then there are classes that teach you about growing both flowers and vegetables. Dancing—from ballet to ballroom—is a great activity for the more graceful among us. And there are a multitude of apps on local and distant hiking trails and parks to take advantage of on beautiful sunny mornings or afternoons.

Depending on how depleted we are, starting Me Care might initially have to be taken in baby steps. We may feel as though we barely have enough energy to begin implementing any Me Care activities. Some may have fought the battle for so long they are continually existing in extreme fight-or-flight mode. In that case, we should be gentle with ourselves. It may take some time to get healthy again. There is no wrong or right place to start. The smallest step is still a step in the right direction when we are working to bring back a measure of normalcy.

We have done our best to supply unconditional love, guidance, boundaries and more for our family. Without seeing success, possibly during the Meantime Phase, it can seem as if all we have done is still not enough. God never expects us to do more than our best—even if our efforts have not been perfect.

I had to give myself the *mirror test* daily. When I brushed my teeth at night, I would look at my reflection in the mirror and ask myself and God, *Did I do all I could do today for my child and my family?* It is quite amazing how often we glaze over the fact that we have done all that we could do in a given day. We often focus on what we did not do three days prior. The mirror test serves to remind us that we succeed far more than we do not succeed—no matter what the circumstances might be announcing.

Our children and their behaviors are not required to have a place in our personal self-image. Our prodigal children do not define us or dictate whether or not we are God-loving people who are doing their best in the world. We cannot take the blame for the failures of our children. It is not a burden worth carrying.

Blame is an unhealthy emotional attachment that results from the trauma we have experienced. It can end up turning into a habit if we are not careful. We often use it as a way to process what our children have done without giving them full responsibility for their actions. We are essentially assigning blame to ourselves to feel better about our child when the only thing that would truly make us feel better is to see them whole and healthy again. Blaming ourselves only serves to beat ourselves up a little more over things that are not under our control. We have got to get over the blame game where our self-image is concerned. The other party participating with our children is Satan. If we need to lay blame, that is where it should go.

The fruit of the Spirit, nine characteristics of the Holy Spirit that can assist us in moving away from blame and furthering a healthy self-image, are found in Scripture. "But the Holy Spirit produces this kind of fruit in our lives: love, joy, peace, patience, kindness, goodness, faithfulness, gentleness, and self-control. There is no law against these things!" (Galatians 5:22–23 NLT).

To separate ourselves from the challenges we are having with our children while still being able to guide them, we ask the Holy Spirit to develop these fruits within us. The goal is to treat our children as God would treat them (and as we want them to treat us) even in the worst moments of their lives. Our aim is to grow in the fruit and make it our natural defense system. As God develops the fruit in our lives, there is no room left for blame or self-berating.

To walk in the fruit of the Spirit, we allow the Holy Spirit, who lives in us and who works in partnership with God, to develop each of these fruits. As children of God, we have an automatically endowed influence—given by God through our behavior in cooperation with this fruit—to shape life around us.

Love

The first fruit is love. We are to strive to love as God has instructed us. "'Love the Lord your God with all your heart and with all your soul and with all your mind and with all your strength.' The second is this: 'Love your neighbor as yourself.' There is no commandment greater than these" (Mark 12:30–31). This type of love is meant to be unconditional. As we face our children in the battle, we can love them unconditionally while not loving their evil behavior. It helps to know what the components of love are.

> Love is patient, love is kind. It does not envy, it does not boast, it is not proud. It does not dishonor others, it is not self-seeking, it is not easily angered, it keeps no record of wrongs. Love does not delight in evil but rejoices with the truth. It always protects, always trusts, always hopes, always perseveres.
>
> 1 Corinthians 13:4–7

Let's face it. Unconditional love is a tall order; however, we do not have to cultivate it alone. God will help us grow and develop unconditional love throughout our lives.

Joy

Joy is one of the most complex aspects to develop in difficult times. It is almost impossible to be happy when our children are suffering. But there is a distinct difference between happiness and God's joy. Happiness is a feeling that is based on circumstances. Joy comes from the heart of God and contains the significant ingredient of hope. There are many times that our children steal our happiness, but their behavior cannot steal our joy. Joy remains because we have decided to put Jesus in control of all our trials. Our joy comes from the confidence that we will find rest in Him.

Peace

When we are continually facing tumultuous interactions with our children, peace can seem highly unobtainable. But like joy, this peace is not the world's peace. The Bible tells us that it is a peace beyond our understanding that we find when we fall into the arms of Jesus and trust that He is in control (see Philippians 4:7). This kind of peace is only found in His presence and power. The most fantastic vacation spot in the world, meeting with our most admired individual, or any other worldly thing will never give us the kind of peace that Jesus has promised. In fact, He promises we can find peace even in the darkest hours. "Peace I leave with you; my peace I give you. I do not give to you as the world gives. Do not let your hearts be troubled and do not be afraid" (John 14:27). Peace is a gift from God. Receive it and see it increase every day.

Patience

We talked about patience earlier and how necessary it is during the Meantime Phase (see chapter 7). While waiting for prayers to be answered and seeing our children's lives turn around, daily life can get very mean. Distraction, discouragement, disappointment and despair can settle in. The enemy fights us the hardest while we are standing firm in our faith and waiting on God to move on our child's behalf. We are so used to going about our business in a fast-food world that it is increasingly harder to comprehend that some tasks can take extended amounts of time. And yet, God works out many things during our long periods of waiting. His supernatural touch is always working to change our lives for the better. Patience is developed the more we exercise it and lean into God.

Kindness

As we fight for our children, we must continue to be kind toward them, to retain our compassion. This is how God treats us. He is kind and has compassion on us even when we are acting in sin. Many times, kindness will be the game-changer for our prodigal. The Bible shares what God thinks about kindness and how to orchestrate it. "Be kind to one another, tenderhearted, forgiving one another, as God in Christ forgave you" (Ephesians 4:32 ESV). This kindness that we express to our children allows them room to make choices and changes that could help them heal.

Goodness

Some believe goodness to be a characteristic of being courageous. We have to be willing to risk rejection and speak in love to our children. We must do the right thing at all costs. The book of Romans explains how important goodness is to our own Christian walk. "Or do you despise the riches of His goodness, forbearance, and longsuffering, not knowing that the goodness of God leads you to repentance?" (2:4 NKJV). We have to be able to talk to our children in God's truth, be prepared to be rejected for it and continue on in transparency with both our children and God.

Faithfulness

Faithfulness can disappear quickly at the first encounter of testing or trials. Standing in what we believe when the world seems to be crumbling is faithfulness. In the warfare for our children, we must remain faithful to God, ourselves and our family. We must be the parent our wayward child can trust, faithful to love even when the behavior is heartbreaking and unacceptable.

Gentleness

In the thick of the battle for my children, this one was a challenge for me. Even so, I have pursued gentleness. Inside chaos and stress, I often found myself coming across as sharp, abrupt and bothered. Although I was speaking the truth, my truthful words were cutting and hurtful. Far from gentle! Although I appeared mad or agitated, I was actually overwhelmed. We must be gentle with our delivery (remember what we discussed in chapter 10 about communication?). As we develop gentleness, we become better listeners, much calmer and have greater understanding.

Self-Control

Self-control, although mentioned last, is key to the other eight. Without self-control, the others would be impossible to exhibit. Self-control requires yielding to God and no longer acting on our feelings or emotions. When we control ourselves and stay out of God's way, He will help us react and respond in ways that will accomplish His purposes.

To develop the fruit of the Spirit, we lean into what we are learning spiritually and allow God to work through us. The fruit of the Spirit is cultivated through the power of God in us.

Picture handing your car keys to a six-year-old and asking him to drive you to the store. Now ask yourself what adult in his or her right mind would do such a thing. Yet we ask the same of God when we do not continually seek to learn and grow with Him. God did not intend for us to remain spiritual babies forever. He desires that we incrementally grow in His ways so that over time He can reveal more and more of Himself to us.

Periodically we should ask ourselves, where is my identity aligned? Do I need to make changes so that I am more like God and can better guide my wayward child back home? These questions constitute an opportunity for us to measure our spiritual growth. If we do not assess periodically what we have learned, we will not know what needs to be done to move forward in Him and His purposes. We are meant to become mature believers and act as such.

By making the effort to reassemble our lives into some sense of normalcy, we are stepping into our full identity. We are deciding it is okay to cease living inside the bubble that only contains child and parent. We are accepting that we are more than parents. We are individuals who have a God-given right to pursue everything God has in store for *our* lives as well. We may not be able to achieve taking a trip around the world today, but almost all of us can start with a good soak and thirty minutes of silence. Enjoy what normalcy you can!

ME CARE MOMENTS

What activities bring me joy?

1.

2.

3.

4.

5.

These are ways I could relax:

1.

2.

3.

4.

5.

Hobbies I would like to pursue are:

1.

2.

3.

4.

5.

WHAT CAN I DO TODAY?

Focus on what you need to do to create adequate Me Care using the lists above.

On an index card, write out the following verse so that you can remind yourself frequently of how important it is to take care of yourself.

A merry heart does good, like medicine, but a broken spirit dries the bones.

Proverbs 17:22 NKJV

A PRAYER FOR ME CARE

Father, thank You for creating me to be whole and healthy. The plan You designed for my life is good, with a hope and a future. Help me to connect with all that You want me to pursue, even beyond being a parent. Show me when I am ignoring my body, mind and spirit, and enlarge my spiritual vision so that I may see how to return to the path of mental, spiritual and physical health. Help me to celebrate You, even through the rough places. You are still fighting the battle as I take my rest to restore and refill. In Jesus' name, Amen.

Evicting Enablement

Steve and I had prayed and prayed. If we were hearing God right, the move from Mississippi to Florida was the right move. This meant that we were going to leave everything we had ever known. We were both born and raised in Mississippi and had never permanently resided anywhere else. This was where we had raised our family. The kids were now 23, 21 and 20. When God gave me this download, He placed in my heart that the transition was to save my children. Moving to Florida would give them all a fresh start, a new beginning. We decided to restart our lives in Florida under God's guidance. So we bought a house in Florida and allowed Steven to live in our condo.

What seemed like a God-given path for our family quickly became an enabling disaster. While we were trying to trust Steven and give him independence, the experiment turned out to be an enabling way to live beyond any boundaries or right choices. Steven immediately got wrapped up and entangled in the vacation state of mind of Florida. In other words, while we thought we were helping build Steven's independence, we were enabling him to party wildly. Sometimes what we, as parents, think of as helping can actually enable our children to dive further into the dark.

After spending years nurturing and taking care of our children, we might have bent and stretched boundaries and rules and otherwise veered off the course of what might be considered appropriate. We have sacrificed for them. We have poured our lives into their lives. And eventually, it gets downright hard to know whether we are helping them get their lives together or enabling their self-destructive choices.

The Faces of Enabling

The definition of the word *enable* means "giving someone the means or opportunity"[1] to do something. Enabling becomes a negative act when we inadvertently enable our children by giving them the means or permission to destroy themselves. There is not one of us who would purposefully enable destructive behavior. But it is a sneaky thing, and it often comes disguised as something else.

One way we can enable our children is by giving them money without teaching them the responsibility of having it or earning it. It starts out in small ways. "Dad, can I have $20 for the football game?" And then it grows gradually until it gets out of hand. All too soon they come to expect that we are their private ATM with an endless, unquestioned supply of cash. We are dishing out cash for anything and everything. "Hey Dad, I signed up for the trip to Europe, and my $1,000 deposit is due tomorrow."

If our children expect us to pay for their social calendar and what they dream up—especially if they are pursuing things that we do not approve of—we might consider how we can cease enabling them. If we are not careful, this money that enables them to do as they please may be the money needed later for rehab, counselors or medicine. When it comes to money, the battle plan for our prodigal children is that we do not exacerbate their problems by paying for their destruction.

To be able to gift our children with the cash to enjoy things is a perk of being a parent; however, the responsibility of a parent is to teach children to understand that accountability comes with money. When you give your daughter twenty dollars to go to the Friday night football game, for example, you expect her to actually go to the game and make good choices while she is there.

As our children get older, we may choose at times to lend them money for something with the understanding that the money will be paid back. Where we often fail is that we do not follow through on the repayment. Helping a child learn to manage credit is another part of parenting. If you lend your child money, be sure to set up a repayment plan. Do not lend more until responsibility is shown.

Another financial enablement is turning our back on a child who is moving from job to job. There are certainly reasons to leave a job. But, if those reasons are not valid, you have an opportunity to teach about commitment and responsibility. Enabling a wayward child to quit jobs often so that he can return to his previous lifestyle of retrieving money from Parents Bank & Trust is going to cause more battles.

Another common enabling action is being the first to rescue our children from the consequences of their disobedience. We have bailed them out of jail, over and over, without expecting repayment in some form. We have paid for tickets hoping to preserve their driving records. We have even taken care of them (multiple times) when they were sick after overindulging at a party. With a long and steady history of rescuing them, we have only accomplished reinforcing their wrong choices by communicating, "I'll always be there to pick up the pieces, no matter what you do."

Motivations

Clearly, we want our children to know that we will be there for them; however, we do not always need to act as their clean-up crew. Notice in the paragraph above I referred to repeated offenses. Addressing a first-time situation in a positive way is to be expected. Consider this: A young child is caught stealing a piece of candy or a small toy. When the parent finds out, she has the child return the item and stands beside him, in loving support, through the consequences. Some parents would say, "But don't all kids do that?" Even if that is true, it does not make it right. Allowing your child to get away with such behavior might set a pattern for your child as he or she experiences bigger challenges. You might be tempted to turn your back—until the action is too big to ignore.

Fear is probably the biggest motivator for enablement. Parents cannot abide the thought of their children getting hurt. Without trying hard at all, we can envision our children driving drunk and hurting themselves or others, ignorantly taking a drug overdose, attempting suicide, acquiring a sexually transmitted disease, getting pregnant and more. I have a friend who once gave me a very valuable piece of advice when we were discussing my son and his behavior. Believe me when I state that he was more than capable of committing any of the acts I just mentioned—and was even successful at a few of them.

"I can't quit thinking about what he's going to do next," I moaned.

She looked at me for a moment and said very quietly, "What if you decided right now to trust God with your son and not think about a broken leg until you actually see it for yourself?"

Stepping away from enablement also means turning our backs on any "what ifs." I had to lean in and believe in this verse with everything that was in me. "Have I not commanded you? Be strong and courageous. Do not be afraid; do not be discouraged, for the LORD your God will be with you wherever you go" (Joshua 1:9). We can walk away and know that no matter what we face or how bad it looks, God is with us.

The diabolical irony of enablement is that we think we are helping our children when we may be allowing them to harm themselves in a greater capacity. This is when we must decide that we can no longer support our children's self-destructive choices.

Finding the freedom to break the chain of enabling is very difficult. It requires a lot of courage and determination. You cannot expect change if you are going around the same mountain in the same way. You must make a change to get a change. The same holds true when we are no longer enabling our children to self-destruct.

Disable Enabling

It is most helpful to define responsibilities and expectations for them. If your teenagers, for example, are to get to work at a certain time and you have made it clear that you will not wake them up for their shift, will you stick to your guns and allow them to oversleep and miss work? Or what if you have decided you are not going to clean their messy room anymore? If they do not keep it fairly clean, what will the consequences be? What about not allowing them to have free rein of the food pantry? Our children are to fulfill the expected responsibilities that have been clearly defined or there will be consequences.

Once our thoughts and rules are solidified, we are ready to explain to our children that we will no longer assist with their efforts to decline and defy. We can also inform them of what they can expect and how they play a role in our new reset. The new routines and rules will be different for all of us. We might implement household duties and responsibilities if they live at home. If they do not live at home, we might announce that we are not willing to pay their bills anymore. The goal of these changes is to show our children we are not going to support immoral choices.

Understand that if we are dealing with children who are on a rebellious path or who have gotten comfortable with our responses, our reset will be met with hard feelings and loud voices. They will be angry. Some may even tell us how much they hate us. They will accuse us of not loving them or abandoning them. Even so, we must stand firm. These comments serve as signs of hope that we are making the right shift. No one ever changes without being uncomfortable. The transition from enabling to helping is harrowing for us as parents as well as for our children. Their anger and angst are a healthy indication that they recognize and comprehend the rule changes.

The hardest words to hear will be "I hate you." No doubt, there is nothing more awful than hearing mean-spirited and hateful words coming out of our children's mouths. It is in those moments that it seems as though our heart is ripping out of our chest. These outbursts are a product of being forced away from the easy way of continuing their destructive habits. We have become their catalyst for change. Most importantly, we are no longer participating in enabling behavior.

We need to make good deposits in our own lives to stay strong and confident. There are many communities where we can find others who are experiencing the same challenges. Supportive groups or communities add reinforcements as we make good shifts in our lives. They provide help and resources we might know nothing about. We can find safe places to share our worries and concerns, and we can receive guidance from those who have gone through similar experiences. Ultimately, we can see that we are not alone in the battle.

One nationwide group is Al-Anon.[2] This is a beautiful community, a mutual support program for people whose lives have been affected by someone else's drinking. By sharing everyday experiences and applying the Al-Anon principles, families and friends of alcoholics can bring positive change to their situations. This can happen whether or not the alcoholic seeks help or admits the existence of a drinking problem. Al-Anon is not a Christian-based community, but it is a place to build friendships.

If you are looking for a faith-based community, Celebrate Recovery could be the place.[3] This organization offers a wide range of assistance beyond what we might need concerning our children. Celebrate lists several areas of help, including addiction, anger, codependency, eating disorders, food addictions, love and relationship addictions, physical, sexual and emotional abuse, alcohol/drug addictions, sexual addictions and gambling addictions. This Christ-centered community bases recovery on God's power.

Many church communities are adept at creating small groups that are specific to the needs of their people, such as those of parents who have incarcerated children. Participating in a smaller church group community may offer some challenges if you are not comfortable sharing your messes with fellow congregants. But finding assistance in a church is much more powerful because God is the center of attention. We should be selective in picking out a group. We need to be sure that the group fits our needs. No group works if it is not a completely safe atmosphere. We should not have to worry about offending others. Beyond groups, it is also possible that local pastors can meet with us.

There is certainly no harm in becoming avid students of the negative behaviors in which our child is acting out. If our child is depressed, for example, we can access quality books on overcoming depression in young adults. We have to be diligent to research the source of such a book, but once we have, gathering as much information to understand our child's problem better is a good thing. Ignorance is not bliss. The more we know about what our children are battling, the more we can fight it with wisdom.

Some of the best sources of inspiration my husband and I found were books in which people shared their testimonies. It was good to hear about their trials and what worked in their lives. There are many self-help books with real-life applications and information to offer. There are many online sources, as well. Many libraries provide online services as well as physical places to find resources. There are great medical websites that deal with many of the topics we face, and there are websites and resources through our government. Part of gaining wisdom is becoming a proficient researcher.

Investing time with God is an essential step in moving away from enablement. The time in each day is valuable and non-negotiable. We only have 24 hours to work with. If much of our energy is spent battling for our children, time seems to evaporate. Before we know it, we are left empty and out of time. Because we are told to take care of ourselves and do what makes us feel better, finding more time to give to God seems like an oxymoron or countercultural.

Then there is the matter of caring for the rest of the family. The hours are eaten up before we have taken our feet off the bed and placed them on the floor. But the Bible has always been the not-so-secret weapon to win against the devil every time. We are told to "seek the Kingdom of God above all else, and live righteously, and he will give you everything you need" (Matthew 6:33 NLT).

This verse represents the assurance that when we are intentional about giving Him our time, we will find so many rewards. Putting God first looks like reading His Word, seeking His wisdom, asking for His guidance, singing His praises and praying to and with Him.

The best money my husband and I spent was for counseling. Seventeen years into our marriage, when the kids were thirteen, eleven and ten, we almost divorced. My husband, Steve, and I lived on opposite ends of the house and had locked each other out of our respective rooms. We loved to hate one another. Our marriage was dead, but we were also desperate for change. We fell to our knees, bargained and begged with God. We asked that if He was real, would He please give us a miracle and help us start over again from scratch? Neither of us was willing to walk away from a seventeen-year investment. God responded and resurrected our marriage.

That was over eighteen years ago. After we invited God to rescue us, we went to work, and that included counseling. I would go Monday, Steve would go Wednesday, and we would go together on Friday. We did this for over eighteen months. We were so poor that we had to put the fees on a credit card, but we made this huge investment into ourselves, our lives and our family. If you are struggling with enablement and cannot get it under control, please consider that you are worth the investment of counseling. If no one will go with you, then make the choice to go alone. Everyone else will benefit, too.

Finding the right counselor may not be a one-and-done experience. Please know that it may take a little trial and error. We should try our best to find a faith-based counselor. Remember, this is a spiritual war over our prodigals. We need a counselor who can help us both spiritually and in the natural. If we feel uneasy with our initial choice, or if we feel that our mindsets do not match, we should not hesitate to find another resource. We can keep searching until we find the right fit. That way, we can build up spiritual weaponry, tools and practical applications to preserve us during the battles.

In an effort to stay away from being enablers, we must guard our eyes, ears and heart. Chances are that we have unknowingly accumulated a community built to aid and assist us in our habits. "Of course, you had to give him the money. What would any mother do?" Friends who mean well often support all our decisions. When we are trying to reverse gears and try different strategies, that support can be a detriment. It is perfectly okay, and even healthy, to explain the details of our struggles to those closest to us and ask that they help us to break old habits.

The more we stay in God's Word and in His presence during our transition, the better. It is the easiest way to hear His voice over the world's noise. Eventually, we will find that our decisions become more manageable. Our lens will become more tightly focused on how God looks at our child and our situation.

Once we understand that a part of the process of stopping enablement includes investing in ourselves, we open ourselves up to the enrichment found in other communities, books and counseling. The more we nurture our mind, body, soul and spirit, the easier it will become to stay away from any behavior we are working to avoid.

When we endeavor to break old habits and take on new ones, our body often suffers from additional stress. When I put forth the effort to step away from enabling my children, one of the side effects I experienced was a body that was riddled with aches, pains and pent-up energy. I got into the habit of setting aside time each day to perform my own form of "praisercise." I had no idea what I was doing other than attempting to combine my time with God and walking. It gave me time to remind myself of God's magnificence and to exhaust my energy in a positive fashion.

The act of praise includes singing, telling of His goodness, giving and confessing. In simpler terms, it means being thankful for God's blessings and showing Him how we feel. I started by meditating on Psalm 9:1–2, Psalm 18:2–3 and Psalm 28:2, 6–7. From these verses, I obtained my praise instructions:

- Praise God for what He has done for us.
- Praise God that He has saved us from our enemies.
- Praise God that we can teach our children and following generations about Him.
- Praise God for His goodness, mercy and grace.
- Praise God for allowing us to demonstrate our faith in Him.

Praise is an outward demonstration of how grateful we are for God and all He has done, is doing and has yet to do in our lives. Praises flow out of the abundance of our heart. When we do this, especially in difficult seasons of our lives, others see God working in our lives. It is a type of intimate worship. Nothing else is as vital as this personal and authentic relationship with God!

In my opinion, there is no more excellent exercise than walking. There are no special requirements and no special equipment needed, other than a pair of tennis shoes. It is as simple as putting one foot in front of the other. When I first started, I was doing it mainly to expend all my excess stress. Pulling away from enablement often left me wringing my hands and not yet knowing where to go or how to act. The added negativity of my children also raised my stress level a notch or two. All that energy had to go somewhere. Little did I know how incredibly healthy my actions were at the time.

The experts at the website Prevention give several benefits to walking. Allow me to share them with you. It improves your mood. Just ten minutes of brisk walking per day can lift your spirits. Walking helps you burn calories and maintain a healthy weight. It reduces the risk of chronic diseases. Daily walking can lower blood sugar levels and systolic blood pressure. There is also a thirty percent lower risk of cardiovascular events (like heart attacks or strokes) for those who walk regularly. I was particularly excited to learn that walking boosts our brainpower, making decision-making easier.[4]

So there you have it! Walking may not be your exercise of choice but find some way to physically release the tension that is wound up inside.

STEPS TO OVERCOME ENABLEMENT

- Learn to recognize enabling behavior by obtaining additional education in books, classes or podcasts.
- Redefine the responsibilities and expectations of both parent and child.
- Accept that there will be conflict, confrontation and anger in the face of change.
- Gather a supportive community within churches or assistance groups.
- Consider individual counseling.
- Invest in positive health habits such as "praisercise."

WHAT CAN I DO TODAY?

The road that turns away from enabling behavior can represent a wonderful change in your life. Write the following on an index card as a reminder that God has already supplied you with everything you need to overcome this tendency.

> And God is able to make all grace abound to you, so that having all sufficiency in all things at all times, you may abound in every good work.
>
> 2 Corinthians 9:8 ESV

PRAYER ON ENABLEMENT

Father, thank You for Your guidance. I do not want to enable my child as I realize this is not a healthy behavior for either of us. Show me how to walk away from activities, conversations and other behaviors that are detrimental instead of healing. Allow me to assist my child in only positive ways through Your instruction. Give me the strength to endure any storms that may erupt as I begin to place particular responsibilities and consequences back where they belong. In Jesus' name, Amen.

PART THREE

DEALING WITH THE ROUGHER STUFF

The Voices in Our Heads

Thoughts of despair and defeat were swirling around and around in my head. *Steven will never make better choices.* Then came, *Lawson is surely going to take a drug and never wake up again.* There was a long season in which the telephone was my worst enemy.

The first of many middle-of-the-night phone calls came when the police stopped Steven. They noticed him as he was driving home because he was running off the road. Police protocol allowed them to start filming from their dash camera to record evidence. When they eventually pulled him over, they began to search his car. We had always taught Steven to respect representatives of the law, no matter what, and tell them the truth.

One of the officers asked Steven, "Do you have any drugs in the car?"

In his drunken stupor, Steven replied, "I gave a girl that I don't know a ride home from the party. She left one Xanax in between the seats in the cup holder." This response would come to haunt Steven for the next twelve years. The police impounded Steven's car, loaded him in the backseat—just like we have all seen on television—and took him to the police station. They booked Steven for DUI and a felony drug possession due to that one Xanax (that was not his) that was nestled between the seats in his car. Shortly after that, the middle-of-the-night phone call came at our house.

Steve, my husband, answered, and I heard him say, "Yes, officer." Then he responded, "I will see if I can meet you with that amount of money." What the officer had told Steve was that they had arrested our son, and if we could come up with 2,400 dollars cash for bail, then they would not have to haul him to prison. The prison system in our area was dangerous and full of murderers.

Part of this middle-of-the-night phone call trauma was the huge question lingering in the air after Steve hung up the phone. Where in the world were we going to find 2,400 dollars cash in the middle of the night? The ATMs would only give 600 dollars per machine. By the time we made the rounds, we were still a thousand short. Then Steve remembered that a dear friend had returned from a trip to Europe the day before. He called him at 2:30 a.m. to see if he still had any vacation cash available. His friend came to our rescue and met us at the police headquarters. We were able to bail Steven out.

One call in the middle of the night is overwhelming for most parents. Over the next few years, we received too many more. There would be calls to tell us that our son had been drinking too much. We received calls saying that one of the children had wrecked the car or had been arrested again. Every time we got one of these calls, my mind would go straight to horrific assumptions. *Oh Lord, the next call will be to tell me one of them is dead.* Every time I heard the phone ringing around midnight, my mind was off and running through worst case scenarios. *Which one is in jail now? Who has been hurt and how bad? Have they hurt someone else?* With every call we received, my stomach would drop to the floor. I would immediately become physically ill with terrific intestinal cramps and diarrhea. It was my physical reaction to devastation.

It seems that when we are tasked with parenting prodigals, our mind naturally goes to an awful and desperate place. Looking back, I realize it was truly heart-wrenching. My default to even a benign phone call was to become frantic and wonder whether my child was dead or not.

Feeding Our Brains

There is a truth that helped me overcome these defeating thoughts and worst-case scenarios. The Holy Spirit helped me to realize that our mind grows based off whatever we feed it. I will give you a picture of what this looks like to me.

What we visualize is located within our brain. The thoughts that pass through our brain are its food. When we feed our brains negativity, the outcome is low energy and weakness. But when we provide our brains with good ideas and positive thoughts, the result is a brighter outlook. I found that when I fed my faith and starved my fear, I was able to break down the debilitating voices in my head. This provided my brain with more positive statements.

When the devil tosses out the bait of life-sabotaging thoughts, we must drop it immediately. We do that by "casting down arguments and every high thing that exalts itself against the knowledge of God, bringing every thought into captivity to the obedience of Christ" (2 Corinthians 10:5 NKJV). The entire concept comes from Paul, the apostle, and he explains why we should do so.

> I beg you that when I come I may not have to be as bold as I expect to be toward some people who think that we live by the standards of this world. For though we live in the world, we do not wage war as the world does. The weapons we fight with are not the weapons of the world. On the contrary, they have divine power to demolish strongholds.
>
> 2 Corinthians 10:2–4

He is referring to the war of the mind and the power resting behind its existence. We cannot allow our mind to run wild imagining every kind of bad situation or the worst outcome. We cannot feed our mind fear and expect faith to grow. We cannot assume the worst-case scenarios and believe for the best at the same time. To do so is, in effect, asking for the thing we fear most to occur. We must destroy any thought that does not align with God's promises and His Word. We must become adept and disciplined in controlling our mind so that we are better equipped for the war over our prodigal child.

When we rehearse the defeating voices over and over, we create a cycle that produces a snowball effect. The name of the cycle comes from what happens to a snowball as it rolls down a hill. The snowball gets larger and larger as it gathers more snow; therefore, the snowball effect describes something that grows in significance or size at an increasingly faster rate. Our negative thoughts become more potent as we allow them to roll on. Every situation, even those that start small, builds up inside our mind and increases in power and momentum as it goes.

Fighting the Triggers

Most negative thoughts get started by a trigger. Triggers generally fall into three categories: emotional, environmental or exposure. Triggers are often based on old routines or cycles, so each person's trigger points are different.

Although the answer as to why we get triggered is not always straightforward, we can try to understand what starts the process. If we are able to, we can work on managing the triggers, which can help keep anxiety and stress from overloading our mental health. In my life, the sound of our telephone ringing in the middle of the night was definitely a trigger point. As I began to try to resist the urge to swim into negative territory, I worked on reminding myself that not every call was detrimental to our household. In fact, we received far more comforting calls.

Part of reversing the voices in our heads is to replace current negative phrases with preselected truth. As soon as I could catch myself wandering through the worst outcomes in my head, I would immediately stop. My replacement thought went a bit like this: *I can't control what our child will decide or do, and I certainly can't control the circumstances that he/she creates. The best thing I can do is to be as prepared as possible. God will help me every day to be ready for whatever comes my way.*

It is worth the time to try to identify what our triggers are and then proactively manage our responses to them. If absolutely no other words can be found in our head, we can incorporate a type of time out and do a breathing exercise. We can pause in this manner until our positive statements come forth. Formulating these practices will eventually begin to slow down or eradicate our repetitive, self-defeating thoughts.

Because of my family's traumatic times, I had way too much practice in panicking. I finally learned to pause and pray. Instead of panicking and allowing my mind and emotions to go out of control, I would attempt to block every emotion. Immediately, I would feel the power of God controlling my feelings, and I would have confidence in God's sovereignty. I knew He was in control over the situation. This was as simple as taking a deep breath, pausing a few seconds and then praying.

> *God, I am scared, and I need You to step in and help me in every area of this situation. Although I am shocked, I am reminded that You are not surprised. You know about everything that happens. God, help me. God, rescue my child. In Jesus' name, Amen.*

These runaway, negative thoughts are self-sabotaging. When I would let my mind run or hang on to one erroneous thought, I was already moving toward defeat. It was self-inflicted defeat, but it had the same effect. Zooming in on one negative area and making it more significant can also keep us down. Jumping to conclusions can also bring us misery and leave little room for a positive result. We have to be kind to ourselves, especially during the transition away from what we have allowed to dictate our thoughts in the past. It is unrealistic to think we can change a deeply ingrained thought pattern overnight.

One of the greatest tricks I have learned to help me change bad thoughts or to limit the impact of triggers is using a rubber band. Every time I get a negative thought or a defeating emotion, I pop myself on the wrist. Another great way to turn around a trigger is to take a time out. Learn to step out physically, and for sure mindfully, and allow ten seconds to pass. This, too, will help you gain perspective and reset emotions.

Journaling can also prove to be very helpful. When we write down what we think, lies become exposed. When they are exposed, we can confront them with the truth, God's Word. You might find it helpful to divide the paper into two sides. On one side, write down what you are telling yourself, and on the other, write out the truth. This helps implement new thoughts more easily. When you can see what is going on in your head, you may find it is easier to adjust those thoughts into a more positive framework. What we think affects how we act, and that dictates whether we are gravitating to the more positive and truthful thoughts or staying in a rut with the old damaging lies.

An Example for Reframing

In an article on VeryWellMind.com, Elizabeth Scott offers a few suggestions for walking through the process of reframing our minds. Let's examine them here.

> The first step in reframing is to educate yourself about some of the negative thinking patterns that may greatly increase your stress levels. . . . The next step is to catch yourself when you're slipping into overly negative and stress-inducing patterns of thinking. Being aware of them is an important part of challenging and ultimately changing them. One thing you can do is just become more mindful of your thoughts, as though you're an observer. . . . As you notice your negative thoughts, an effective part of reframing involves examining the truth and accuracy (or lack thereof) of these thoughts. Are the things you're telling yourself even true? Also, what are some other ways to interpret the same set of events? Which ways of seeing things serve you better? Instead of

seeing things the way you always have, challenge every negative thought, and see if you can adopt thoughts that fit your situation but reflect a more positive outlook.[1]

We can reframe our mind by attempting to eliminate the thought immediately. The moment a thought or any other enticement from the enemy appears before us, we must stop it and ask God to help us push it away. My favorite Scripture verse says, "We demolish arguments and every pretension that sets itself up against the knowledge of God, and we take captive every thought to make it obedient to Christ" (2 Corinthians 10:5). The moment a thought or anything that is contrary to God comes into our mind, we must cast it down immediately. We cannot give life to anything that is in conflict with God.

When I quit smoking, for example, the enemy would tempt me to smoke a cigarette. The demon would wait until I was at my most vulnerable point, usually tired and weak, and say, "All you need is to smoke one cigarette and you will feel better and less stressed." What if I had allowed myself to visualize taking a cigarette out of a pack? What if I had then seen myself lighting up the cigarette and smoking it? I would surely have succumbed to the temptation. I always knew that I would have to immediately kill the thought. I would tell the devil he was a liar. I would thank God that He had freed me to be a nonsmoker for the rest of my life. We can all apply this process of casting down any thought that is not of God so that we can keep our mind focused on the goodness and hope of God.

In practical terms, planting more positive, truthful statements in our mind will help us replace the old thoughts. When we do this, we will see negativity be overridden more often, and we will start to look at things primarily through a positive mindset. When we are tackling a challenging situation, instead of feeling defeated, we can say to ourselves, *I've got this with God on my side. He is bigger than any problem I face. This will all turn out to be fine.* Changing the way we think opens the door to receiving a positive outcome. It has been said, "I've had a lot of problems in my life, and most of them never happened."[2] We must make sure that we maintain a positive mindset. Rarely does what we worry about actually happen.

By choosing to break the cycle of fearful and defeating thoughts, we are declaring that we are not going around the mountain again with our wayward child. Defeating the voice in our head automatically creates a greater boldness that allows us to step into the battle in a different way. This is a critical step, and it is not easy. Changing the way that we think can be harder than it sounds. Many of us have fallen into the enemy's trap of speaking the wrong words over our own life and the lives our children.

We are meant to create life through our words, as God demonstrated by speaking life over us. When we declare God's Word, when we speak God's promises over ourselves and our family, and when we use the power of God to fuel our mind, we can more easily keep hope alive for our prodigal child.

HEARING HIS VOICE

There is absolutely no reason that we should believe that we cannot hear and obey the voice of God.

"My sheep listen to my voice; I know them, and they follow me."

John 10:27

"He who is of God hears God's words; therefore you do not hear, because you are not of God."

John 8:47 NKJV

Your own ears will hear him. Right behind you a voice will say, "This is the way you should go," whether to the right or to the left.

Isaiah 30:21 NLT

And this is the confidence that we have toward him, that if we ask anything according to his will he will hear us.

1 John 5:14 ESV

WHAT CAN I DO TODAY?

Once we retrain our minds to accept the Word of God over our thoughts, we become even more fit for the battle. Add this verse to your index cards to revisit His power.

For the word of God is alive and active. Sharper than any double-edged sword, it penetrates even to dividing soul and spirit, joints and marrow; it judges the thoughts and attitudes of the heart.

Hebrews 4:12

PRAYER TO HEAR GOD'S VOICE

Father, thank You for continuing to reveal the path that my family is to travel. Help me to push aside my own thoughts and listen to You. I am blessed to be able to hear Your voice in my hour of need. With You, God, I believe that anything is possible. I know You can retrain my mind in ways that honor You and benefit my family. In Jesus' name, Amen.

The Comfort of Community

Throughout the course of pregnancy, it seems as if we inherit an automatic community. From the first announcement of the exciting news, people from far and wide begin to surface. I had no idea how many friends, family and neighbors desired to engage with us frequently during the pregnancy and birth journey of each of our children. When I think back, I can see how the buzz started prior to their births.

Months earlier, close friends and family began to try to guess what sex the baby would be. Today, it is not uncommon for expecting parents to throw a huge party to reveal the gender of their baby. As the delivery date was estimated, plans began for the baby shower. I received calls from those who wanted to purchase special gifts for our bundles of joy. Family and friends gathered at the shower to celebrate, rub my belly and suggest names for the soon-to-be-delivered baby. My excitement built as my bulge got bigger and bulgier.

As a matter of fact, my tummy got so big that it intrigued my scientist-at-heart husband. Steve wanted to measure just how big I was, so he proceeded to scrounge around the house for a tape measure. He carefully pulled it completely around the diameter of my baby bump. It turned out that I was one inch bigger around than I was tall!

I found it interesting that as soon as I learned I was expecting, I suddenly felt as though I had things in common with other people with whom I might have previously not had much to discuss. I also became acutely aware that my mom, other parents and other pregnant women had all shared in this blessed experience. Society in general seems to appreciate our temporary condition. People smile and are kinder to us as they recognize that we carry a baby inside. Strangers help us load our groceries, they open doors for us and some even bend down to help us pick a dropped item up.

Then the curiosity of birthing protocol begins to nudge us. We want to know all the details of delivery and the various aspects of the baby growing within. That calls for a trip to the bookstore, where we purchase titles such as *What to Expect When You're Expecting*, or something similar. As soon-to-be parents, an overwhelming wave of responsibility hits home.

The importance of community is suddenly visible. We start to see how the strength of our circle of friends relates to our ability to thrive as a family. There will be all kinds of meetings that parents traditionally attend. If our children are enrolled in daycare, our social circle will include caretakers and other parents who send their children to the same location. Perhaps we might join the lactation community where all the women share breastfeeding tips and support.

As our children progress from Pre-K to Kindergarten, we begin to widen our social circles and activities even more. In this stage, our children start their extracurricular lives, adding sports, art, music lessons and more. We become coaches and snack coordinators. We carpool with other parents to help cart the kids back and forth to practices and games. This process of ever-widening community continues right up to the point that our child takes a hard left turn into territory where no one wants their children to go.

As our children persistently make self-destructive and hurtful choices, fewer and fewer options for community remain. In truth, they have already tried, or even succeeded at, courting an entirely different set of so-called friends. At this point, we can begin to feel as if we are stranded on an island. The more our children get into trouble, the smaller our community gets. We no longer have anything in common with the parental community in which we have been for years, and it becomes lonely and isolating.

Honestly, as parents uncover more and more sad truths about their children, most are too ashamed or embarrassed to talk about the traumas that may be going on at home. Isolation, combined with zero transparency, leaves us all scrambling to keep it together mentally and emotionally.

The Hazards of Isolation

The topic of isolation was magnified during the COVID-19 pandemic. The new attention given to loneliness has been bitter-sweet. Loneliness has been recognized as a real threat to our well-being and general health for much longer than quarantines, but there have not been many solutions.

For those raising prodigal teens and young adults, you may have found that the isolation of the pandemic made life even more hellish. Even if you had found a group that kept your issues confidential, they would not have been able to meet due to COVID restrictions. Even our healthy teens and young adults suffered tremendous emotional distress during COVID. After sharing isolation and loneliness with the rest of the world, the solution remains the same. The only way to combat loneliness and to help our children is to find appropriate communities that can support us. We need to build a tribe to be able to thrive.

The right community can sometimes serve as the glue that keeps things together; however, as we struggle to figure out how to manage our broken child, we often find that the energy it takes to think about joining others can seem insurmountable. Facing the painful emotions that we are dealing with, and then sharing our realities with others, can serve as a major obstacle to finding and joining like-minded people. Let's unpack the importance of community when we are in the battle fighting for our children.

We have talked about it before, but it is always good to be reminded that the enemy prowls like a lion to devour our children and us (see 1 Peter 5:8). Satan wants us to be isolated and feel alone, and he has used that as an excellent tool against us. The lies the devil fed me were relentless. Satan would provide thoughts such as: *No other parents are dealing with out-of-control kids like yours. You can't share what Steven did, or else you will be blackballed by everyone. If you are such a great Christian parent, why are all three of your children failing so miserably?*

The enemy knew exactly what to feed my mind so that I would remain quiet in my suffering as my children were spiraling down. These self-condemning thoughts came straight from hell and kept me in isolation way too long. I finally became so desperate that I started to seek out others who were facing the same issues. I invested in communities where I could move past the pain into a purpose for my own life.

Science has tested and recorded that the emotional strain of loneliness can cause real physical issues: sleep disorders, heart disease and a weakened immune system. Also, isolation can be a high-risk factor for premature death.[1] These are all excellent reasons to consider community essential.

There is no doubt that communities offer support and safety when people are feeling tired or confused. In essence, the encouragement of others can help to build us back up. When hopelessness sets in, community represents a fantastic resource to help fight off negative feelings. Most of us need to feel a greater sense of belonging. We prefer to feel as though we are a part of something bigger than ourselves. It is wise to locate others who share similar values, interests and views.

Acceptance into a group satisfies one of our greatest needs and helps give us a stronger sense of self to cope with life in general. It is possible to find the extra push or accountability to stand tall and move through our circumstances. With the right community, we are influenced to be healthier and not fall into unhelpful habits or thoughts. When we struggle to keep ourselves straight, the right community can help us stay on task. Community motivates us to invest in our well-being, and it brings positive changes to our lives.

Sharing activities, ideas and feelings with others reinforces our sense of self and benefits our overall mental health. Sharing truly is caring.

Miscellaneous Communities

There are several types of community that will offer various benefits for our well-being. The basic criterion for these communities is that they should all have a positive atmosphere that reflects our beliefs and morals. That is how we will find the necessary avenues to be strengthened and encouraged and to remain hopeful. We also need to consider communities for our children. The value of a positive community is the same for adults as it is for children.

We can start by finding others who have similar beliefs in God. We need to zero in on a few personal preferences, as well as the preferences of our children, before we begin our search. Many churches offer more than one style of worship to appeal to both the younger and older congregants. As with most things, we have to be proactive and do our research. And we need, of course, to ask God to show us and lead us to the place we need to join.

There are a couple of commonly held traditions amongst churchgoers that are not particularly helpful when you are picking out the best community for your family. You have probably heard them before. "I go to this church because it is right down the street from my house." If we own a properly working car or can navigate the bus routes, there is no reason not to venture further for the sake of building quality community.

Another frequent justification for attending a particular house of worship is, "My family has been going to this church for thirty years." If our legacy church is meeting the needs of our family, there is certainly nothing wrong with continuing the tradition. If it is not, that is another story entirely. There are many denominations from which you can choose.

Traditional liturgical or contemporary services? Modern praise and worship music or classic hymns? Affiliation with a specific denomination or a non-denominational church? Small congregation or mega church? We should hone in on what we really care about. Any facet that does not matter to us allows us to remain open-minded and possibly expand our options.

As we visit different churches, we need to shift our focus to how the community affects us and our spiritual desires. We need to make sure that we feel as though we have things in common with the members. We need to assess if the community is service-minded. Are they focused on where we think God may be calling us to serve and minister? Giving back is just as important as receiving. Do they have a healthy view of the pastor and people? Do they seem to work together well? Be intentionally nosy. All of these details matter. When we find our spiritual home, we will share our talents, time and treasures with those in that specific community. We want that to be a successful and smooth transition.

Another benefit of finding an appropriate church home is that other believers will likely have gone through and overcome similar trials through their faith. Testimonies might be shared on how God brought healing even in the midst of pain. As we get to know the people of this group, we might find comfort as they share how God made a message out of their messes.

Our children can receive benefits, too. There could be Sunday school classes for their age group that could open doors for them to make friends with other children. Many times, this group of friends is quite different from their school friends. They will be learning about God and, hopefully, be sharing these thoughts with the other kids. Many churches have ministry opportunities for junior high and high school students, which create even more positive ways for our kids to have fun and learn about God. The idea is to have resources available for when our children are ready to avail themselves of them.

Through new relationships, we can exchange wisdom and gain greater insight into how to manage our lives in better ways. We can often plug into small groups that are designed to help meet a specific need. Gathering with a group of men and women who are the same age and *not* discussing children but exploring God together can be an exhilarating experience.

As I look back at the darkest hours while parenting my prodigal children, I realize that I did not get as connected with communities as I probably should have. I cannot help but recognize that there are so many benefits to joining a community versus remaining utterly separate and dealing with what is going on in our children's lives in isolation. It may not be an easy step for some, but it is essential to get us through our misery. I eventually learned the advantage of being part of a solid community. I was able to build relationships that had no bearing on children. These friendships have enlarged my social circle and helped in many new ways.

One other place we can seek out community is to look at our passions. If we love art, there are museums that need docents or that offer classes. Or we can engage in group sports such as a bowling league. For readers, there is the possibility of joining book clubs—both in person and online. We can think about activities that we enjoy so much that time flies. The advantage of engaging in a passion group is that we know that we will have at least one thing in common with the other participants in the group.

When connecting with new communities, it is critical that we remain our true and authentic selves. It is easy to "fake it until you make it," but this will not work. We must be willing to be honest about the good and the bad parts of both who we are and about parenting our prodigal. If we continue to hide our story, we are not operating in honesty. Telling the ugly truth includes becoming vulnerable, but that helps us to build deeper relationships.

We also need to ensure that those with whom we interact are as genuine as we are attempting to be. We can ask God to bless our friendships. We can also ask Him to show us which relationships are good for us and which we should not pursue or need to gently distance ourselves from. Typically, most of us do not have much spare time, so we need to make sure that we maximize our efforts. We should visit groups or communities that are focusing on what would benefit us right now.

Added Perks

Extended time spent in one community brings added perks. We begin to quit worrying about the opinions of others concerning most any topic—including our children. We start to see that everyone makes mistakes and that no one is perfect. We might find the courage to get rid of toxic relationships that are preventing us from growing. We have the potential to break free from our prison of fear, because we have learned to face our fears by hearing the stories of others. We become nicer, kinder and feel good about being a part of something bigger than ourselves.

Often, as a direct consequence of interacting with fellow humans regularly, we begin to exchange our old selves with newer ones. Our self-care takes a higher priority, along with the pursuit of putting positivity first. As we move deeper into communities, we leave behind old mindsets and immense negative emotions. We are depositing newfound hope into our lives and generating proactive measures so that we can keep moving forward.

EXPLORING COMMUNITY NEEDS

I would like to have the following in my church environment:

1.

2.

3.

4.

5.

I believe my child(ren) would like the following in a church environment:

1.

2.

3.

4.

5.

WHAT CAN I DO TODAY?

Battle the devil's tool of isolation by reaching out to a community. In the meantime, write out this verse on an index card to remind you of what God has to say about community:

And let us consider how we may spur one another on toward love and good deeds, not giving up meeting together, as some are in the habit of doing, but encouraging one another—and all the more as you see the Day approaching.

Hebrews 10:24–25

A PRAYER FOR COMMUNITY

Father, I know You designed us to be in relationship with one another. Help me find places where I can grow, learn and love. Teach me how to be vulnerable with others so that they can help me in my weaknesses. I know that we are meant to gather in fellowship with other believers to love and support one another. I ask that You show me a church community that is good for my entire family where we can give back in Your name. In Jesus' name, Amen.

15

Sleuthing

onitoring our children in healthy ways is the goal for all parents. It is rational to observe our children's behaviors and moods day in and day out, and take note of any unusual emotional extremes. This could include almost any emotion that is over-exhibited for an extended period of time. Long-lasting negative emotions such as sadness, depression or unusual silence might indicate that it is time to seek outside help. Conversely, children who are extremely elated without reason might be using enhancements (such as alcohol or drugs) to retain their joy. It is the parent's job to notice these things. We also benefit from getting to know the friends our children are close to and who they hang out with often. This can be an enjoyable experience for everyone.

It is natural for parents to monitor their children's money. It is good to know how much they are spending and where they are spending it. Parents should also know how much time their kids spend scrolling on social media and what they are browsing online. Being aware of these behaviors allows us to open conversations with them, and having awareness of how they are spending their time helps us implement better boundaries for them.

Even in a healthy child's life, parents can help establish limits and boundaries that keep them from getting hurt or being lured into harmful situations. When a teen begins to date, for example, parents help them by showing them the importance of physical and emotional boundaries so that they can continue to pursue a healthy dating relationship.

Parents can have discussions about how godly people behave within a dating relationship and what their children should expect. Conversations about what the characteristics of a godly lady and gentleman are, as well as what God prefers, are excellent to have. Because of these conversations, the new couple may take it upon themselves to add rules of their own, such as deciding that they will not participate in public displays of affection. Or they may decide that they are not obligated to share passwords or things of this sort.

When our children were in high school, for example, the annual fall homecoming dance followed a high school football game. After the dance, the parents provided a breakfast party. The homecoming breakfast usually occurred very early in the morning (around 1:00 a.m.). It was our way of filling up empty bellies before sending the students home to bed. Many parents were fine with these activities. They had not previously had any trust issues or rules broken by their teens, so they were willing to let them travel late at night and stay up until the wee hours of the morning.

In healthy families there is seldom any hesitation to allow children to go and do as they please. As long as trust has not been violated, parents allow their sons or daughters to spend the night in the homes of people that they really may not know well. Because trust is still intact, they are willing to take their child's word. They may ask their child for the household phone number and reach out to confirm that this is a legitimate invitation.

Unfortunately, these sweet times of trusting can be crushed in an instant. Let's look at when Mary, who had been dating a boy for several months, began to become more sexually involved. The boundaries her parents had put in place were quickly fading. Then one month she did not start her period. She was so upset. Finally, she went to her mother and then to the store for a home pregnancy test. They performed the test, and Mary was indeed pregnant. Everything from that moment on changed both the parents' and Mary's lives forever.

Boy, do I get it. My children continued to break my trust over and over. My life felt like a roller coaster from hell. I know you can relate to this, too. I grew so weary of summoning the courage to think my children were finally in a healthy state and making better choices. Then the roller coaster would take a ferocious drop, creating the terrible decline in my stomach as my emotions fell back down into the valley of misery. This is where we immediately start looking for newer ways to gain control over our children. Some of us even resort to spying on our children (or sleuthing) in an effort to keep the shock of the roller coaster lifestyle to a minimum.

As we are fighting the effects of our children's backsliding behaviors, we are also fighting against the roller coaster that having access to certain technology brings. This access has lured this generation into sin more than ever. Bad choices are now only a click away. Watching porn can happen with the tap of a few keys. Buying drugs is a social media app away. Hanging out with the wrong crowd can be an instant option.

There are many more things our kids can get into now. If we were to dial the clock back to the 1950s and 1960s, we would see how children's lives were so different. The homes we lived in never had to have the doors locked. Even at night there were rarely any safety concerns. Our cars would have the windows rolled down and remain unlocked. Kids might be gone from home all day, but they were mostly on foot. The only mandatory time to arrive at home was dinnertime. One phone and one television for everyone in the house to share—and that is if you were lucky enough to have those. Furthermore, parents stood together. If Mrs. Smith saw that Johnny was up to no good, either his mother got a phone call, or she chastised him on the spot—or both.

It is hard to find any similarity to those nostalgic days. Our children today are one click, one taste, one step and one choice away from death. Almost every child in America has a phone that they call their own. This phone holds the enticement of any bad choice you can imagine. Click. Lie about your age and get access to any porn one desires. Click. Friend a guy on Instagram who was recommended by another friend and open the door to any drug you want on demand. Click. A child predator begins to groom your child. Click. What other dark, yet unimagined holes are out there? Technology and television have made the world a cesspool, a devil's den for any of our children.

Strangely enough, this new world of technology has also empowered parents to spy on their kids as they have never been able to before. We have almost been forced into the responsibility of monitoring what goes on inside our homes. Some say it is sleuthing, but we can call it spying, too. Technology provides parents more ways than ever to follow our children, read their texts and see what they are doing on social media.

Master Sleuthing versus Communication

It is almost as if we are in training to be Sherlock Holmes' sidekick, Watson. We are attending master sleuthing school. Sherlock had his pipe and his magnifying glass that he used as he was busy detecting clues. He was always the best at finding out what was really going on or what the real answers to problems were. Following in Sherlock and Watson's footsteps, we are looking for tidbits of information about our teens and young adults every chance we get. We pull out our magnifying glass and open our children's phones and Instagram accounts as often as we are able. The only thing we are missing is the pipe.

Spying or sleuthing may seem like the correct response for parents who are continually at risk of having their hearts shattered because of a child's destructive nature. The challenge resides in how far we take it and what this detective work does to our countenance. The mysteries we are trying to solve might actually represent rules we should be setting. Sleuthing (or spying) is exhausting business—even for Sherlock!

Let's look at some evidence that can help us decide if we are striving to be Watson. We drive by the house where our child said she would be hanging out to make sure she has told us the truth. We create an account on Instagram pretending to be a friend to get our kids to befriend us. We sneak a peek at our child's phone that was left accidentally on the kitchen counter so that we can read his or her texts and jot down phone numbers to check out later. We enlist others, such as our child's friend, boyfriend, girlfriend or sibling to join the master spy club and report back to us if alcohol or drugs are used. We must go to God and ask Him how much is too much.

One of the lowest seasons in Steven's life was when he was in his mid-twenties. I had become friends with many of his friends and exchanged cell phone numbers with them so that I could keep track of his activities. At one point, I texted some of them in the middle of the night to find out where Steven was partying. On other occasions, I texted them to ask how much alcohol he had consumed. I was constantly trying to investigate and gather clues about Steven's destructive behaviors.

When I look back at that season, however, I realize that most of the information I garnered was either useless or made me feel even worse about what was going on in his life. I see now how much sleep I lost in the pursuit of being able to tell myself that I was doing something valid for my child. In reality, all of my activities were about making me feel better. There are dangers that we will certainly fall into if we infringe too much on our children's privacy. Let's take a look at what a few experts have to say on the matter.

An article published on the Nautilus website addresses this issue. They interviewed Sandra Petronio, who is a professor of communication studies and the director of the Communication Privacy Management Center at Indiana University–Purdue University, Indianapolis. "Privacy isn't just important for adolescents. . . . It is their duty. 'An adolescent's main job is to individuate, to move away from being controlled by the parent. One very clear way they do that is in their demand for private space.'"[1] Intruding on a kid's privacy damages the relationship between parent and child. "When parents snoop, they show mistrust. That overarching need for control really damages the relationship."

The article continues, "Unsurprisingly, when kids do not feel they can trust their parents, they become even more secretive." Skyler Hawk, a social psychologist who studies adolescent development at the Chinese University of Hong Kong, saw this effect. He followed a group of junior high kids in the Netherlands. "The researchers asked the kids about whether their parents respected their privacy. A year later, the children of snoops reported more secretive behaviors, and their parents reported knowing less about the child's activities, friends, and whereabouts, compared to other parents. 'We can trace a path over time from feelings of privacy invasion to higher levels of secrecy to parents' reduced perceptions of knowledge about their children,' Hawk says. 'If parents are engaging in highly intrusive behaviors, it is ultimately going to backfire on them.'"[2]

It seems to play out that good communication with your kids is more effective than snooping on them. It is possible to be open about putting tracking applications on your kids' electronics. If they agree to be tracked, then open communication can be established regarding what they are up to. If knowledge about your kids is garnered with their knowledge, then you can freely chat about their friends, their activities or their mental and spiritual health. Communication in this manner allows for an open and respectful relationship.

Helicopter Parenting

There is another detrimental parenting behavior into which we can fall. It is called helicopter parenting. It is named as such after parents who hover over their children like a helicopter that is ready to swoop in with its guns at the first sign of any danger for the sake of the ground troops. Although we often enact this behavior to protect our children, it can lead to many negative outcomes. In doing so, we provide very little room for our kids to gain the healthy separation they need to grow into adults.

Many times, we do not allow them to fail at anything, including sports, academics and relationships. We make decisions for them that they should be able to make themselves. Under the pretense of "knowing what is best," we override any desires our children have by choosing what sports we want them to play, what area of study they should take or what college they will attend. We can overstep healthy boundaries and end up over-disciplining and over-correcting our children.

To counteract our desire to hover, we need to take time to examine our behavior. Are we helping our kids with tasks they are capable of doing on their own? Are we shadowing our kids or monitoring their social media and online exchanges in a healthy way? In today's world it would be almost negligent not to know where our kids are going online and on social media. There are many dangerous lures and evil predators that we as parents must protect our kids from by establishing safe boundaries; nevertheless, monitoring should continue and be age appropriate, and it should not make our children feel as if we do not trust them.

Many parents have opted to design a customized contract for their teens and young adults concerning social media. This gives the parents and children a way to negotiate privacy and protection. The contract, for instance, can include passwords and updates on their social media accounts. In addition, a clause can be added where the child agrees that he or she will not set up fake accounts.

Negotiated, periodic checks on activities and posts are usually included in the contract. The agreement should state that if at any time the parent feels the child is at risk, the parent will automatically take the actions necessary to attain safety. Contracts help keep the child from feeling as though his or her privacy has been invaded.

Parental Negatives

Sleuthing in the extreme can have a negative impact on parents. The greatest foundation for any relationship is trust. When we go beyond healthy monitoring of our children's activities and step into spying or helicoptering, we can completely destroy trust with our children. This can cause our teen or young adult to be more inclined to hide more things from us, keeping us further in the dark.

As I shared earlier, I felt as though I was the master when it came to spying on Steven. What I did not realize was that the girls who were his friends betrayed me. They told Steven every time I texted them. They shared the nature of our phone calls with him, too. Then these girls acted as though they did not know where Steven was, when, in reality, they were with him at the time of the conversation. They kept all details of his drinking to a minimum and tried to make things seem less harmful than they were. All the while, I had no idea that they had exposed me and were purposely not telling me everything about Steven's out of control behaviors.

Needless to say, my experiences with Steven's friends led me to a false sense of security. What I was told was not the truth, and yet I chose to believe it. After I realized what was going on, my anxiety actually increased. I became swept up in how much I had missed through that time period.

The outcome of sleuthing can be terrible for both parent and child. The goal is to help our children responsibly manage their social media contacts, their online participation and their in-person social decisions. Our hope is that we can teach them a healthy and self-monitored lifestyle that will continue into the future.

After our prodigal children break our trust, it can be a natural default to begin monitoring their behavior secretly or to hover over them making decisions that they can safely make. We have seen how this can lead to unfortunate and sometimes debilitating outcomes. We must dig deeper and trust God with our wayward children like never before. We must realize that no matter how much control we try to execute over our child's life, it can have a tragic rebound effect. We must limit our sleuthing and spying because it will only lead to more disappointment and a false sense of security.

SLEUTHING OR NOT

I currently monitor my child in these areas:

1.

2.

3.

4.

5.

I moved into extreme sleuthing when I:

1.

2.

3.

4.

5.

I need to sit with God about this:

1.

2.

3.

4.

5.

WHAT CAN I DO TODAY?

Sleuthing to an extreme is all about self-awareness. God intends us to seek Him to know where our boundaries should be.

On an index card, write out the following Scripture verse to remember that we all have boundaries and are responsible for maintaining them.

> But if we judged ourselves truly, we would not be judged.
> 1 Corinthians 11:31 ESV

A PRAYER FOR EXTREMES

Father, please help me hand over to You all of my behaviors and actions concerning my prodigal children so that they can grow—even if it means that they experience negative consequences. Help me to lean into Your arms so that I can find rest when I do not know where they are or what they are doing. I am grateful that You see everything. Please continue to watch over and protect my children. Thank You for supplying my family with Your wisdom and provision. In Jesus' name, Amen.

16

Handling Outside Information

We had finally found a way to keep Steven from getting into trouble during his senior year—we grounded him from everything. As soon as we got through the adjustment period for this new setup, we received all kinds of advice from various people.

It was strange, because we suddenly felt as if we were on a stage in front of family members and friends. Although most of them seemed to have our best interests at heart and did not intend to hurt us, I found it tough to take. The most challenging interaction I faced was with my parents. They did not understand the spiritual warfare tactics I was attempting to implement.

My mom and dad successfully raised five children. Their parental journey began in 1954 when my oldest sister was born. As you might imagine, my parents had zero experience with technology and the demons that could attack our children through it. The entire time my children were making critical, life-threatening choices, my parents would lovingly chime in without truly knowing how to help. It was no fault of their own. They had sweet intentions to help guide us through terrible dark seasons.

Friends also offered unsolicited advice. I remember an instance vividly where my friend advised me, "I wouldn't allow him to start driving again quite yet." This comment came on the cusp of another round of grounding. Steven had come in too late one night and had broken his curfew. We grounded him a month for punishment. It was Steven's first infraction around ignoring when he was supposed to be home. He seemed to have learned his lesson. He was compliant and agreeable most of the time, even while he was grounded. We felt as though he would think twice before deciding to come in late at night. And yet this friend insisted, "You should ground him longer than a month." Ironically, this advice came from someone who did not have a teenager. She had no clue what challenges we were struggling with.

The first line of defense for unwanted advice is to carefully guard our response. The best answer comes when we are managing our reactions. For me, this usually means that I should immediately hit a pause button. I often respond very passionately, and many times it is mistaken for anger. It is for me, however, simply a dramatic response. It is perfectly okay to avoid overreactions by gathering your composure in silence for one or two minutes. Once you have managed your reaction by breathing and pausing, you are in a much better position to comment appropriately.

Empathy is the ability to feel and understand the emotions of another. As my friend later acknowledged, she really did not understand the underlying emotional battle that we were going through. When things in life are hurting us and the stress is overwhelming, we begin to truly know what it is like to battle. Our feelings are often very raw and real. If a person does not recognize what is going on, chooses to ignore what is happening or has not had a similar experience, they cannot possibly acknowledge the pressure and the pain that is piling up. And we cannot expect them to recognize those issues. Most of the time, the people who are around us mean well, but these good intentions can lead to adverse outcomes. Who wants to hear advice when he or she is barely surviving?

In one instance, we had been up all night trying to get one of the boys out of jail and settled back at home. By the time all was said and done, we were drained both physically and emotionally. We certainly did not need a well-intended neighbor coming over and telling us what she would have done in the situation. She was older and felt it was her duty to tell us all her various viewpoints on the intricacies of the situation. By the time she had finished, the only idea we all entertained was how we never wanted to have to talk to her again.

Then we realized she had no idea how exhausted and spent we were. She had not meant to be a busybody. We eventually understood that she was attempting to help us. We replied to her unwanted advice with a generic comment that we would let some time go by and reassess what punishment was appropriate. Although we did not want her to be offended, we were not terribly worried about her feelings. In the moment, we only had our child's best interest in mind and at heart.

Handling Outside Information

As parents, we are not responsible for how people who give us unsolicited advice react to our comments; however, that does not mean that these moments are an opportunity for us to blow off steam. We still have to deliver our point of view appropriately. But if they take it personally, it is okay to let them walk away. We cannot afford to add more drama to the battle at hand.

We need to conserve every ounce of energy and emotional capacity that we can because our kids need us. We cannot get caught up in whether or not the person delivering the unsolicited advice is negatively affected if we do not take his or her advice. It is a given that we want what is best for our children, and we will pursue any solution that is at our disposal from any source that is viable.

When unwanted advice is given to us, we can install some previously agreed upon boundaries to deal with it. It helps to solidify the intentions and motivations behind the comments. Is this individual giving unwanted advice because they have had experience with what we are combatting? As Atticus Finch from *To Kill a Mockingbird* told his daughter, Scout, "You never really understand a person until you consider things from his point of view . . . until you climb into his skin and walk around in it."[1] No one can know what we face unless they have battled for the sanctity of their child, too. If we find someone who has, we might choose to set aside a time after our emotional roller coaster has subsided to visit quietly with them to see if they have wisdom to offer.

It is also possible that someone who is freely giving advice is trying to make themselves feel more powerful. If we realize that this is the case, then we can choose whether or not we will validate them. In a couple of short sentences, we can thank them for their thoughts and then let it go. Creating boundaries in the form of limiting responses is beneficial to keep tension to a minimum. Boundaries help keep emotions in check, which in turn helps us eliminate unnecessary outbursts in our conflicts with our children.

Let's go back to our neighbor who told us what she would do with our child who broke curfew. I realize now that if I had prepared in advance to receive comments such as she gave us, it would have made all the difference in the world. It took a little practice before I got the system down. Now, if the neighbor says, "I would ground him for at least two months," I would reply, "Well, that's an interesting thought. I will consider that time frame." Another reply could be, "Thanks for that idea. Let me think about it." If a person continues to give unsolicited advice ad nauseam, we can often change their gears by changing the subject. If worse comes to worst, we can simply be blunt. "Thank you, but we need to change the subject."

Before I learned how to deal with others, I experienced times in which I thought my head might explode—there was such emotional pressure brewing inside of me. My blood pressure was high, my heart was beating fast and my emotions were all over the place. If I had to describe myself back then, I would say that I was a pressure cooker that was approaching the moment when the whistle or bell would signify that I was cooked!

Without boundaries and a set of responses in place to deal with those who give unsolicited advice, we are likely to have a nervous breakdown or a cosmic, emotional explosion from which we cannot recover. We must stay calm and cool. We certainly do not need another battle in our lives. The more we refuse to take others' opinions personally, the more successful we will be when we offer our prepared responses and walk away.

It is very difficult to be in control of our reactions when we are at maximum stress and under attack. What is even tougher, though, is when the people closest to us begin giving their opinions and unsolicited how-to advice as it pertains to our struggling child. We often are hardest on the ones who are closest to us, especially in times of darkness.

Even your closest family members can become outside influencers. It never failed that my husband, Steve, and I would argue in the midst of the chaos we were experiencing. We mostly did this during the teen years of parenting Steven while he was making critical life-and-death choices. Our son's actions were almost guaranteed to instigate war between us.

I was the baby of five children. My husband was the oldest of three children. My parents were married until my dad passed away at 81 years of age. Steve's parents divorced when he was thirteen. Their divorce greatly affected him and contributed to the temporary self-destructive path he took as a teenager and young adult. These few differences in how we were raised often created conflict and confusion. But we slowly learned how to get on the same page. We realized we had to be on the same team if we were going to successfully manage our prodigal. We were not opponents, and we had no need to fight against each other in our efforts to make our child behave. We were both on the side that desperately needed to win.

Whether it is our mate, a close family member or a friend, we all have been influenced by others. Sometimes this influence can lead to inner-circle tension and can flow negatively to our children. As we all know, navigating our prodigals through their storms is hard enough without having internal disagreements about how to manage the problems.

Parenting Styles That Serve as Outside Information

Parenting styles can be classified into three categories. Authoritarian parenting, permissive parenting and neglectful parenting.

Authoritarian parenting can produce overly obedient children who may need someone to tell them what to do as adults. *Permissive* parents usually have no boundaries and are more worried about creating positive self-esteem for the child. *Uninvolved* parents are just plain harmful. They offer no support, and they themselves struggle socially. These parenting styles are not set in stone. A parent may recognize they are negligent and make changes to correct his or her behavior. It is not hard to see how any combination of parenting types will have its own set of learning curves. Here are some examples of common clashes.

Authoritarian versus Authoritative

These parents may disagree about how much affection they are to give their children. They may argue over whether or not to punish a child, when punishment is necessary or how severe punishment should be. These parents may also disagree about whether or not they should give rewards for good behavior.

Mom says, "My child should be seen and not heard, and it is simply my way or the highway."

Dad says, "I want to explain the reasons behind the rules and take Roger's feelings into consideration when enforcing them."

Authoritative versus Permissive

Permissive and authoritative parents may agree about the need for love and affection, but they may have strong disagreements about which rules to enforce and how to enforce them. Authoritarian and permissive parents may disagree over if and when punishment should happen. Permissive parents might even view authoritarian parents as abusive.

Meanwhile, authoritarian parents may see permissive parents as neglectful.

Mom says, "There are no excuses for your behavior, and you will pay a price for your disobedience."

Dad says, "Kids will be kids, so give her a break."

Permissive versus Uninvolved

Permissive parents want to give their children a lot of love. Uninvolved parents may want few or no substantive interactions with their children. This may cause the permissive parent to feel overwhelmed by the care they must provide.

Mom says, "I know this punishment will hurt your feelings, but it won't last long. Here is your consequence."

Dad says, "It's all right. You don't need to be punished."

Authoritative versus Uninvolved

Authoritative parenting is high-effort parenting. It offers significant guidance and much affection. Uninvolved parents may prefer to stay on the sidelines. Parents who differ in this way could encounter ongoing conflicts.

Mom says, "The reason you have to stay in your room is because you broke this particular rule."

Dad says, "I don't have any real rules, so go do what you want."

Differences in parenting styles are just one point of potential conflict for parents. Conflicts can also stem from cultural values, beliefs about social norms or political views that may lead to significant parenting disagreements. Some parents, for example, allow children to have phones before the age of ten, and others do not allow this freedom until they are thirteen. Some parents grew up going to church, while others never attended. There are many facets worth discussing when it comes to getting in agreement with each other regarding how to parent our children.

No matter what we are addressing in the way of unsolicited advice, the most significant step is to hand it over to God. We must allow Him to move through every detail so that we can understand how He would handle these situations. When we invite God to step in and take over, we can successfully navigate others and move past the moment without spending vital energy we need for our children.

Gossip and Tattling

Let's address the final topics of gossip and tattling. One of the most hurtful things people do when children are caught in doing wrong is to talk about it. Some even begin to add untruths to the details. They start to dramatize every element of the mistake and then build a story that is not totally true. Their stories are often juicy enough to be spread as rumors. Even our parents might be tempted to tattle to us about their version of what our child is doing wrong. It can feel as if they are refereeing our parenting decisions.

There are different ways we can respond to gossip, and it usually depends on the motive of those sharing their news with us. If we perceive that the information is being communicated without malicious intent, we might not respond. But we also must be prepared to relationally maneuver gossip from those who are closest to us. When a close friend or family member is gossiping, we have the opportunity to let them know how we truly feel about having to fend off unnecessary comments. The same rule we discussed earlier about having a set of prepared responses can be applied. The choice is always ours.

We are in a spiritual war and are doing our best to take all the proper steps toward healing. Sadly, when it comes to handling outside information, our friends, neighbors and family members may feel obligated to share their advice and opinions. This can make us feel as if we need to respond in kind. We can always take a time out, consider the source, prepare in advance statements of reply and have those statements ready to deliver as needed. We should take a Christ-like approach, and then hand it all over to God.

PREPARED RESPONSES

This is a good place to practice what you will say to others who give unsolicited advice.

1.

2.

3.

With whom am I having challenges in this area, and what is my prayer for them?

 ## WHAT CAN I DO TODAY?

Most of the people who supply unsolicited advice mean us no harm. We should freely forgive them. Write the following on an index card, add it to the others you have created and recite it at every opportunity:

"And when you stand praying, if you hold anything against anyone, forgive them, so that your Father in heaven may forgive you your sins."

Mark 11:25

PRAYER FOR HANDLING OUTSIDE INFORMATION

Father, please help me to be prepared to give a calm, kind reply to any unsolicited advice. I want to be more like You when I am tempted to be offended. Show me the motivations behind the words, and help me to respond with only forgiveness. Please help my spouse and me to open our hearts and agree on a solid plan to raise our children. I trust You in all things, and that especially includes guiding me in how to be a better communicator. In Jesus' name, Amen.

When the Worst Happens

Most parents agree there is nothing worse than losing a child. Sadly, for some of us, this horrible nightmare becomes a reality. One of the most tragic parts of the spiritual war over our children is that there will be casualties of war. Losing a precious child is the most difficult part of this journey. My heart breaks with every parent I meet who has lost his or her child to these battles. I cannot imagine how incredibly strong they have to be to carry on. One of the greatest tragedies that is unfolding is the loss of so many of our children to suicide, fentanyl poisoning and depression. The numbers defy description. How do we continue to fight the battle of spiritual warfare when the worst happens and we are left with the overwhelming grief that tears our life into shreds?

From an Expert

Rick Warren, a God-fearing man who has helped millions find their God-given purpose and the author of *The Purpose*

Driven Life shared the following in an interview after his 27-year-old son committed suicide.

> We can't handle pain unless we understand there is a purpose. The gospel doesn't offer painless life on this earth, but it does offer us meaning, which makes pain bearable. The first stage was shock, which is a human emotion. Sometimes I'd be sitting at home at night, expecting him to walk in through the door and watch TV with us, as he often did. Then it went to sorrow, which is a godly emotion. The Bible says, "Jesus wept." The only reason you are able to grieve is because God grieves. The Bible makes it very clear; we were made in his image. The third phase is what I call struggle. All the "why" questions. The biggest one for me is, "Why didn't you answer the prayer I prayed every day for 27 years?" The prayer I prayed more than any other prayer went unanswered. But explanations never comfort. What you need in tragedy is not an explanation, you need the presence of God. Then you come to the stage of surrender. Surrender is when you say I'd rather live and walk with God and have my questions unanswered than have all my questions answered and not walk with God.[1]

How do we make sense of the pain caused by outliving our children? Living with the knowledge that our child has gone before us is not something we ever envisioned God designed for us. Rick Warren shares, "When things happen to you, they become part of your life message. It doesn't replace my life message, it just adds to the mosaic. It's another piece that's been added."[2] No one can comprehend the depths of grief of losing a child unless they have experienced this ultimate, devastating tragedy.

This chapter is for those heroic parents who are living beyond their child's death and choosing not to give up the fight of faith. As we face the reality that not all of us will see the victory for our children on this side of heaven, we can attempt to process the pain. Together we can find meaning and make the pain easier to live with.

The Stages of Grief

There are many emotions that play out as we deal with grief. Mourning the loss of a child is a process, and though the stages of grief are the same, we all react differently. Grieving is painful and often can take a long time to understand. We all find our way to mourn; it is a very personal process. Grief is traditionally known to be divided into five stages. They can be processed in any order and more than once. Follow along as we take a closer look.

The first stage is *denial*. People in this stage say things like, "This can't be happening." In this stage, our lives cease to have meaning. We are full of shock and disbelief; we are paralyzed with pain and fear. This stage is a coping mechanism that helps us survive the loss. As we become more stable and more substantial, we experience the next stage.

The *anger* stage is necessary to begin healing. People ask, "Why is this happening to me?" Many believers struggle with being angry at God, but He is bigger than any anger we have toward Him. We must feel the anger regardless of who or what is its actual focus. Processing anger becomes a catalyst to healing that builds strength. When we feel all alone in our pain, processing our anger helps. One of the incredible characteristics of God is that His love for us does not change—even when we are mad at Him. His compassion for us does not waver. God is bigger than our anger, and He will love us through the grieving process.

A friend's child died young. This friend was shocked, was full of questions and yelled at God for taking his child so early. Then one day as he was crying, he heard God's voice say to him, *Do you want your child to leave heaven and come back to earth? I am watching your child be happy, laughing and whole, and the young one walks with Me every day.* He cried tears of gratitude and thanked Him for showing him that his child was in a better place. He had confidence that he would see this child again when he left his days here to reside in heaven.

Milestones may increase our anger for a while. As we begin to face the reality of never seeing our child again, there can be a sense of being robbed of what was due to us. The overall injustice of why his or her death should have never happened can cause us to seethe. We realize that he will not be blowing out birthday candles. She will never wear a cap and gown or receive a degree. We will not celebrate a wedding or grandbabies. These are some of the most brutal realities that parents will have to face. And they are justified in their anger over the loss of these events.

The next stage is *bargaining.* "God, I will do anything to change this." We start making deals with God about how much we will serve Him. Or we begin to tell God we will do anything to have the life we had with our child back. The "if only" statements closely follow, especially when we begin to blame ourselves. We relive moments where we feel that if only we had done something different, our child might still be alive today.

Often, bargaining is accompanied by a large amount of misapplied guilt. It is something of a relief to finally recognize that we can do nothing to bring our child back. There is nothing we can exchange with God, and there is no plea from our sorrow-filled heart that will negotiate an avenue to bring our child to his earthly home. With God's help and grace, we can settle our mind and emotions around the thoughts of how our child is far happier in heaven than he or she would have been with us. We have to try to wrap our heads around the fact that God Himself is celebrating our son or daughter, while we are down here longing to hug them one more time.

The next stage is *depression*. We ask ourselves, "What is the use of living without my child?" This is where we meet our pain and deep sadness head-on. Depression is ubiquitous in this stage. We may wonder if the sadness will go away and the will to live will increase. It would be unnatural not to respond to the tremendous loss we are experiencing. Depression is a necessary step in the grieving process.

One of the surest ways to get through depression is to go to counseling or group therapy. Counseling allows us to work one-on-one with a therapist to process these sad emotions. Also, counseling can help determine if we need medication for sleep problems or other issues associated with depression. Group therapy is precisely what it says. Several people who are dealing with depression due to loss meet together to find comfort or solutions. Group therapy can be a lifeline as we connect to others who are walking in the same shoes that we are. Having a group of others who can identify with us and who share similarities is often helpful to be able to survive the most devastating phases of grief. Sometimes there is no clear solution or immediate way out of the tunnel, but utilizing these three tools can help.

Eventually, we begin the *acceptance* stage. We acknowledge what has happened and realize that we cannot change it. Then we seek and develop ways to cope with our grief. This is not to say that we are all good about what has happened to us—no parent will ever feel right without their child; however, we can begin to manage our lives in a new way. We learn new ways to live without our children.

There will be a tug-of-war of emotions as we walk closer to healing. We may feel as if we should not have a good day without our child. But somehow, we should give ourselves permission to heal, feel and enjoy things again. There is no doubt that having a child pass away is traumatic. It is not conducive to the design of life we are accustomed to seeing. We are supposed to live to a ripe old age and have our children outlive us. The loss rocks the very foundation of what we thought life would be like. But through God's grace and mercy, we can traverse this very difficult trial to fulfill the purposes He still has for our lives.

Grief Affects Everyone

The death of a child affects the entire family. Everyone is devastated. Sadly, this can make it hard for other children to get the support they need. Brothers and sisters are the first friends our children have in the world. They live together and play together. When a sibling passes, those who remain have to learn how to navigate their lives in a new way.

Siblings are supposed to be with the family forever, and when they are not, our kids will wonder how they will make it without them. Siblings suffer from all the future memories disappearing. Many times it is necessary to get added support for siblings who are facing grief, simply because parents are battling for their own survival at the same time.

We can help siblings who are grieving in a few ways. We can validate their pain and loss. We can continue to call their sibling by name when talking about him or her. We can find time to be with the remaining siblings one on one and pour positive emotions on them. If parents are unable to navigate the grief of a sibling, it is wise to reach out to a trusted friend, pastor or organization that specializes in adolescent grief.

If we are married, it is time to give our mates some grace. We all grieve differently, and it has an impact on every area of our life, including our marriage. We may need to hold on to our mate more than ever, or they may need to be left all alone. This is one of the most significant traumas a parent and a marriage can face. We must be patient and support one another with our best efforts to get through this painful, unexpected journey.

God did not design us to lose our children; however, He is very familiar with the incredible pain that accompanies the loss of a child. God birthed Jesus, His only Son, so that He could one day die a brutal death on a cross at Calvary. He forfeited His Son so that we would be reconciled with Him. God knows the struggle of watching our children suffer. God sees and knows everything in our lives, and He weeps with us.

There are those among us who run away from God because they are angry that He allowed this tragedy to happen. They wonder, "Where in the world was God when my child passed?" These are natural initial reactions. But the Bible shows us plenty of examples of loss and suffering by God-fearing people. My go-to example is Joseph.

Joseph was a good person. He loved the Lord. But he suffered for years at the hands of his siblings who eventually sold him into slavery. He later became very successful in Egypt, even becoming the second in command (see Genesis 37, 39–41). The lesson in Joseph's story is that God was with him throughout everything that he went through. God protected him from harm and provided ways for Joseph to excel, regardless of the circumstances in which he found himself. The same is true for believers today. God is always there—even when, in our brokenness, we run away.

In other instances, we may feel as if God did not save our child because He does not love us. Or we believe that we deserve this hell because of sin or mistakes in our lives. None of these suppositions are true. God would never intentionally harm us. He would never punish us by allowing bad things to happen to us. As we have explored, there is evil in the world, and death is part of the darkness.

The most profound comfort to be found while in this intensely painful heartache is to know God's promise to us: "And He will wipe away every tear from their eyes; and there will no longer be death; there will no longer be sorrow and anguish, or crying, or pain; for the former order of things has passed away" (Revelation 21:4 AMP). One day we will all be in heaven with our Creator. He will wipe away all our tears. We will no longer feel the sting of death nor the pain of loss. Our mourning will end, and God's extravagant love will envelop us. We will live in a new place in a new way.

There will never be a day on earth that we do not experience the pain of missing our deceased children. Our only hope to be able to live on is found in God. We need to process our grief and allow ourselves to go through the stages to move forward. God will be there to comfort us and keep us strong. Our child would want us to keep living and not just exist. We can begin to work through each challenge until we get to the other side and into our final home in heaven.

PRAYING THROUGH GRIEF

As we let grief take its course, we let the Word of God comfort us.

> "Blessed are those who mourn, for they will be comforted."
>
> Matthew 5:4

> He heals the brokenhearted and binds up their wounds.
>
> Psalm 147:3 NKJV

> Then Jesus said, "Come to me, all of you who are weary and carry heavy burdens, and I will give you rest."
>
> Matthew 11:28 NLT

> "So also you have sorrow now, but I will see you again, and your hearts will rejoice, and no one will take your joy from you."
>
> John 16:22 ESV

WHAT CAN I DO TODAY?

As we move through the grief process, it is vital that we continue to remind ourselves where the source of our healing resides. Add this verse to your index cards as a reminder.

> My flesh and my heart may fail, but God is the strength of my heart and my portion forever.
>
> Psalm 73:26

PRAYER TO MOVE THROUGH GRIEF

Father, I know that You know the worst has come to pass. I am swimming in a sea of emotions and desperately need Your steadying hand in my life. Show me the way through this path of grief. I need You to renew my purposes in my heart and spirit. I ask that You heap Your blessings of peace and comfort upon my family. In Jesus' name, Amen.

PART FOUR

STARTING OVER

When Change Comes

One of the most fantastic moments for parents is when their prodigal child finally gets to the point where they want to change. It does not come easily, quickly or without a lot of stops and starts.

Before we get to the point of victory, we will likely experience some painful disappointments. We may see some glimmers of hope that include positive changes in the choices and actions of our child. It may look as though she has gotten back on track with her life. Our confidence in him begins to build. But then, one unexpected day, we find out that our hope has been crushed as our child makes yet another self-destructive choice. We again ask if we will ever see our child restored. Will we ever know when the change is genuine and lasting?

A most significant heartache while battling the devil over Steven's alcohol abuse came during his senior year of high school. He had been in trouble for alcohol abuse way too many times to count. We were so happy he was finally a senior, and we thought that maybe with him being so close to graduating and getting ready to go to college he might straighten up. He seemed to be back on track. We were so hopeful.

During the fall of his senior year, Steven attended one of the first football games on campus. He had driven after dinner to be there by seven. We assumed all was well. But around eight, we received a phone call from the on-campus police. They were notifying us that they had apprehended Steven and taken his keys because he was stumbling while attempting to enter his vehicle. Once again, our hopes were dashed. We were devastated as we drove to pick him up. We were grateful to God for the intervention of the police and that Steven had been prevented from driving drunk, but we were overwhelmed that he had backtracked again.

A Study from Recovery.org

How many attempts at recovery does it take to attain sobriety? I began to research this question. The information is very scarce, but the few answers I found are very encouraging. The Recovery Research Institute surveyed a large representative sample of adults who indicated that they used to have a substance use problem but no longer do. As part of the survey, participants answered the question, "Approximately how many serious attempts did you make to resolve your alcohol/drug problem before you overcame it?"

The study found that attempts at recovery are not as many as once calculated. Those with five or more years of recovery reported that on average it took five attempts to achieve recovery. Those who had a diagnosis of depression or anxiety or who had received recovery support services (inpatient, outpatient, mutual help, or any support service) reported a greater number of recovery attempts. Interestingly, the age that the problem surfaced and the primary substance used were not associated with differences in the number of recovery attempts before the problem was resolved. This study showed that the average person in the United States who struggled with an addiction to drugs or alcohol took only two serious attempts to achieve problem resolution. The number may be substantially lower than most people might have guessed.[1]

Repeated Attempts Are Common

If our teens or young adults are living with habitual self-destructive behavior, they may require repeated attempts at breaking the habit before the habit actually is broken. Some of our children, for example, get hooked on drugs. These drugs can range from smoking pot to crack. Other kids continually miss school. They act sick and avoid going to classes. Many of these children skip school while we still think they are in class. Children are delinquent with schoolwork. Their grades can suffer intensely to the point that moving forward into the next grade may be compromised. Some kids refuse to submit to the dress codes at school and either face punishment or returning home on a regular basis to gather the appropriate pieces of the uniform.

Every household has its issues when it comes to being at odds with their teens or young adults. In any of these infractions, our children can exhibit a start-and-stop mode of operation as they work toward fixing their problems for good. It may take multiple attempts for our children to fall back in line and stay in compliance. Backsliding is the challenging part of the "I've changed" roller-coaster ride. But it is so much easier to deal with if we know what to do when it arrives.

By this time in the journey, we have been lied to or betrayed many, many times. These are still the child's mistakes and are not a consequence of our parenting skills. Remember, our prodigal children have the power to choose. The fact that they have bothered to notify us about a change lets us know that they know right from wrong.

When we start to see a turnaround in our children's behavior, we can easily reignite our hope that this phase of our family's life is over. We can be tempted to reset and return to the old dreams we had for them. Sometimes, though, we can do this too quickly. Since we never stopped believing that they would return to who we know that they are, we hope that they have learned their lesson and that they understand that the entire family has paid an immense price in consequences. Surely they will not go back to their old habits. We dare to hope that we are done with that miserable, failing chapter of their lives, and we are more than ready to rewrite a much better outcome.

But we must not kid ourselves. Our children must learn to work through and transition out of their battles. We cannot overreact. We must stay calm and as relaxed as possible. When we react in a heightened emotional state, the situation elevates, emotions run too high and everyone can experience damage. Trying not to overreact can seem impossible because their relapse seems to hurt worse after they have had a good run. Naturally, our hearts are aching. We must guard ourselves against overreacting and doing anything we may later regret. The biggest danger we face is sending our child back into the eddy of darkness that he or she has been struggling to get out of.

Take a pause. We can either physically remove ourselves to gain composure, or we can count to ten so that we have time to gather our emotions. We should also watch our tone of voice. It is often not the words we say but the timbre of our voice that delivers our message. In the heat of disappointment, it is natural to take on a condemning cadence; however, we must stay away from this type of emotional giveaway.

Then we wait it out—again. Our child is old enough to make correct decisions. They can choose to overcome destructive behaviors and find support from sources other than parents. We are not responsible for their rescue. Our children must take into their own hands the responsibility of their recovery. We need to remind ourselves of these truths so that we can protect ourselves from the roller-coaster ride of our prodigal's journey into complete healing.

What is so amazing about God's ways is that often He has already lined up appropriate people to support them. People outside of a child's normal bubble can step in and serve as a conduit for God's presence. It is incredible what a hug or a smile can do for our children when it comes at just the right time and from the right people. God is more than able to draw people into their lives, and He has already pre-planned for others who can help our kids return home. As they walk their healing journey, we must pray that God would send the right people who can escort them back into God's loving and waiting arms.

Our responsibility in this process is to encourage our children to accept help. It is appropriate to open conversations up in which we let our children know that they need additional support outside of what we can provide for them. We can share that we see definite signs that they desire to change, but we also see that they need more qualified and experienced help. We can ask them to describe precisely what they want to change in their lives. Do they want to quit drinking? Do they want to stop using drugs? Together, we should make a plan that encompasses what type of support would bring the best path for success.

Once a recovery route is set, we need to find ways we can help support the change. Maybe we pay for the transportation to and from the therapy. Maybe we pay for a residential treatment facility. What is important is that we support their decision to change their lives for the better—but only to a certain point. We have to keep tight boundaries around how we help them so that we will not fall back into enabling them again.

S.O.B.E.R.

I read an article that contained the following acronym to help remind someone working through recovery to keep from acting on impulse.[2] It has stayed with me, and I hope it will stay with you. The acronym makes it easy to understand how our children have a simple way to make good decisions after recovery.

The letter S stands for *stop*, which gives our children a second to regroup. The letter O stands for *observing* and assessing what is being experienced and felt. The letter B reminds our kids that it is time to *breathe*: inhale and exhale in long breaths to slow down their thinking. Then E represents *expanding* one's awareness and remembering where previous bad choices led. The letter R stands for *respond*. Our prodigals need to remember that they can respond mindfully and that they do not have to live this way.

Seldom is there a quick fix for our children. Their journey can be a lifelong one that will ebb and flow. There is no one-answer-fits-all solution. There are absolutely no easy answers. But there is a truth in the Word of God that will always hold certain for all of us. "Even if good people fall seven times, they will get back up. But when trouble strikes the wicked, that's the end of them" (Proverbs 24:16 CEV). We are assured that if we keep our hearts and lives in God's hands, He will certainly help us to get back up again. Another great truth that comforts the soul reads, "The LORD will hold your hand, and if you stumble, you still won't fall" (Psalm 37:24 CEV). God will always be there to rescue our prodigals, and He will help empower them and hold their hands as they walk out their recovery.

An intentional pursuit of God during this journey is our only guarantee for tremendous success, both for our prodigal and for us. Nothing and no one can heal our prodigal except the love and touch of God; therefore, our whole defense against the roller-coaster ride of recovery is that there is hope in God. We may not see a quick recovery, and there may be several attempts to get back up before everyone finds a place of healing, but we know that nothing is impossible with God (see Matthew 19:26). We must never give up the pursuit of God's healing and life-transforming touch as we journey with our prodigal into recovery.

All three of my children finally found healing, but they each had a unique journey home. They all had to fail a few times before they found victory. After many disappointments and broken hearts, we were able to declare that the enemy had lost the war over my prodigals.

In Steven's life, God used an Uber driver in the middle of the night. When Steven was drunk and high on drugs, he experienced the presence of God so strongly that he fell to his knees on the floorboard of the back seat, smothered and pressed by God's Spirit. This tangible manifestation of God's power was the beginning of God delivering Steven and an end to the demons tormenting him.

Lawson was in a demonic attack for almost 24 hours. The principalities of darkness were trying to physically kill him. Steve and I had to witness this full-on, traumatic demonic attack, and we all were forever changed. The devil was defeated at the end of this final war for Lawson. From that point forward in Lawson's life, he said, "I will never lose hours in a day where I have no idea what I was doing or saying." To this day, Lawson has remembered every second of every day and has been fully set free and whole.

During Kaylee's senior year in school, her choices of running with the fast crowd were crushing her. She also had other traumatic issues she was trying to manage on her own. One day, as she was in a friend's car hysterically crying, she said, "I am so depressed that I don't think I want to live anymore." Her friend immediately asked Kaylee if she could pray for her. Kaylee and her friend prayed for God to show up in the car and to help comfort Kaylee. God came to Kaylee's rescue.

She describes it this way. "I was sobbing and was so down that I didn't see any way I would ever find happiness again or have any hope for healing. Then, in the prayer, we were asking God to touch me, and He touched my heart so profoundly that my tears immediately stopped and all of the weight on my chest was lifted off." This one touch from God changed Kaylee forever. She is now thriving, greater than she dreamed or imagined.

I hope the most encouraging takeaway from this chapter is that changes can be achieved. Complete healing and recovery can be realized in the lives of our prodigals. When our children say they have changed and then they fall again, it does not mean that it will remain that way forever. We need to prepare ourselves for the bumps and bruises. Eventually, there will come a day when we can help to educate them and support them in finding their healing. As we have seen through the research, it may take a few times to land on healing ground. Also, recovery happens in its own unique, God-specified time. God's timing is always right on time. As we stay intentional with God in our personal lives, and as we battle against the devil's plans for our prodigal, we can find healing. One touch from God can change everything.

LOOKING AT RELAPSE

It helps to know the emotional signs of relapse.

1. Isolation and a sudden desire to skip meetings or therapy.
2. Poor hygiene.
3. Irregular sleep schedules.
4. Abandoning routines that are part of the recovery plan.
5. Binge eating unhealthy foods.

If my child falls into relapse, I will encourage myself in the following ways:

1.

2.

3.

4.

5.

WHAT CAN I DO TODAY?

Relapse is not an eternal setback. It is merely one more leg of our journey in the fight for our children. Write this final verse on an index card to inspire you not to give up.

"But you, be strong and do not lose courage, for there is a reward for your work."

2 Chronicles 15:7 NASB

A PRAYER CONCERNING RELAPSE

Father, thank You for my increased faith today. I now have eyes to see that You, Lord, can do the impossible. Please continue to guard my heart as my prodigal walks down the healing journey, and help me when my faith is weak. Show me how to love my prodigal as You love them. I pray that they find Your healing touch soon, while I remain ready to partner with You in battle under the power and authority given to me by Jesus Christ and the blood that He shed for my entire family. In Jesus' name, Amen.

Summing It Up

We are in war, but not with our prodigal teen or young adult. Our supreme foe is the devil. Somewhere between our children's birth and where we are today, evil has attempted to take our children captive. Maybe up until now some of us have tried everything and have children who are still barely surviving. The dreams we had for our children have been stolen and replaced by the shock that takes over when we first found them chasing a "fix" or battling suicidal thoughts. We may have originally thought it was a physical battle, but now we know the truth. This is a spiritual war with demons who are seeking to kill and destroy our children's lives. But the good news is that we have also discovered that God has given us everything we need for victory. We now have a battle plan and warfare strategies in place.

This unseen battle is waged against our children through the world's lure of darkness and demons that rummage around looking for a perceived next victim. We must stand in the gap for our children as we seek a new level of faith and a deeper presence of God in our lives. We know the answers, weapons and battle plans can only be received through God's only Son, Jesus. We have learned to feed our faith—and not our fear—through reading God's Word and praying. We now walk boldly through God's power and know we are in partnership with Him. We have what is necessary to battle for the sake of our children.

We have discovered that God's army contains angels. There is a hierarchy of varying types of angels who are all ready to support us in battle. When our children succumb to the lies and influence of the devil, we may not recognize them anymore. We begin to feel defeated and hopeless. But we know that when we choose to partner with God, we can fight in His strength and in His power to defeat the dark army. When we do so, the devil has to leave our children alone. Demons have to flee because, in the end, they have zero chance for success. God is continually fighting battles on our behalf so that the enemy will never see victory.

We now understand who we are and whose we are. We know and fully appreciate our identity. We are God's children, a part of His army and warriors for His Kingdom of light. We are fighters who are fully equipped with armor that is provided by God. From our head to our toes, we have the exact protection that is required to win every battle against the darkness of Satan. Understanding who we are in Christ keeps us winning every time. God guides His warrior-parents in the battle and provides the path to deliverance.

We will become better prayer warriors for our children. The more we pray and spend time with God the more confidence we find. The greatest not-so-secret weapon we have is the authority that God has given us. We have full authority and command over the enemy, so we are able to win consistently over the dark army. We will not lose hope and will strive to stay diligent in battle for the sake of our children. Even Jesus was tempted by the devil and proved how, with God's Word, we can knock the enemy down. When we get battle weary, we can speak God's Word, pray to Him often and know without a doubt that He will deliver our children from evil.

We have seen what a superior weapon prayer can be. We understand that if we are not praying for our children, no matter what their age, there might be no one else who is engaged on their behalf. Knowledge, wisdom and protection are found whenever we petition God. We are continually reminded of the life-saving power for our children and our family that is found in the blood of Jesus. As we pray the blood-soaked paintbrush prayers over our children's lives, we have supernatural protection from the devil and his demons.

We will have to face a Meantime Phase in the battle with the devil. The best defense in waiting for our victory comes through the Three Ps. As a reminder, they are *patience*, *perseverance* and *perspective*. We will have to trust God as never before as we wait on Him to move on our behalf. We will have to stay fierce and not give up, persevering until we receive a touch from God. Then we will have to keep our perspective focused with an eternal lens that provides hope for healing. When we speak, our words must be life giving. We cannot allow anyone to speak words of defeat around us. As God is working behind the scenes, we will actively wait on Him to move heaven and earth for our children.

In our battles with the enemy, we have developed a different kind of trust. When we are absolutely worn out and feel as though we will never see victory for our prodigal, we have to dig in deep and trust God completely. Once we know who God is and understand His unconditional love for us, we can begin to trust Him with a new confidence.

God is nothing like us. He is our Father and our heavenly Dad. God deserves this special kind of trust because He has shown us that He loved us in our darkest moments of sin. The devil lies to us and tries to convince us that we are too far gone for God. But He will never love us any more or less than He does right now. His love has not wavered since before we were formed in the womb. We are always able to lean on Him. God protects, provides, rescues, keeps us safe, loves us at our worst and continues to be our heavenly Father regardless of what we face.

A significant advancement in our battle plan against the enemy is to hand our children over to God. When we realize that our children are God's creation and belong to Him, we are able to release them into God's care. We practice relinquishing control over their lives and allowing God to take over. During those times when we are fighting fear, we remind ourselves that God is the pilot of our children's lives and that He will land them safely and exactly where He intends. Giving God full ownership of our prodigal proves that we trust God to give us victory.

We have practiced initial responses to aid in communicating better with our children. We have thought through how to pick our battles and avoid emotional outbursts over things that are not worth the fight. We jump in instantly when our children are in danger. We acknowledge that we make mistakes, and we now see the benefit of being transparent with our children and offering apologies whenever it is appropriate.

We know how to separate from our children so that we can preserve ourselves, which further equips us for the long haul.

We have explored new ways to face the truth and to choose healthier lifestyle options. We take care of ourselves by finding activities that will replenish and revive us again. We have relieved ourselves of blame concerning our children's self-destructive behaviors, and we are steadily developing the fruit of the Spirit in our life.

We are no longer the rescue-on-demand for our children, deciding that we are no longer going to enable their bad behavior in any shape or fashion. Regardless of the backlash that our children send our way, we will press through. We will be a catalyst for our children as they consider making choices to find healing. We are invested in creating our new self. We have become intentional about the time we spend with God on a daily basis so that He can supply us with life-giving energy and wisdom. With our new self and God's help, we can envision the victory for our prodigal.

We have learned how to win the war inside our own head. We do not allow self-defeating thoughts to take us down. We have discovered how to take every thought a prisoner of war, not allowing our thoughts to hurt us. We write down thoughts that are negative and replace them with God's truth. We are turning bad days into good ones simply by winning the battle inside of our mind. We no longer are going around mountains the same way. We are aware of the enemy's mental bombs, and we detonate them harmlessly by covering them first with the promises and words of God. We declare victory for our prodigal because we know that what we say aloud brings power to the outcome.

We have overcome isolation, and we no longer live all alone on an island. Support from groups, communities and churches has filled our lives. These relationships are true and authentic, allowing us to share the most vulnerable parts of our lives. We encourage and cry with each other. Our lives have begun to reap the benefits of creating a new sense of belonging within several different groups. We have friends and believers who are supporting us in church. Now there are others to help hold our arms up in battle when we get tired.

We have learned to set ourselves free from the pursuit of knowing every detail of our children's lives. No more snooping, spying or sleuthing to the extreme. We have broken away from the false sense of security that is created by trying to find out the secrets of our prodigals. We cannot continue to let their lives and choices consume us. No matter how many lies we find our children being party to, there will not ever be a one hundred percent way to monitor our children.

We now gauge the advice people give us on how to raise our prodigal. We know that they may truly care, but they can never completely understand our specific heartache and pain. We have prepared polite answers for them in advance. We now know it is not worth overreacting as it can add more drama to our already-troubled lives. We have decided not to bother with the crazy stories that have been created about our family members because it is all gossip. When we are warring with the devil over our children, we do not have the energy or time to allow people to distract us or disappoint us. All that matters is that we get our prodigal child back on track so that he or she can be free.

Overall, we have covered a lot of territory toward equipping ourselves for the long haul in the battle for our children. On a personal level, we have, hopefully, realized that our own care is just as important as anything we do for our children.

I would like to share a heartfelt message before we close this book. If you are a parent or a loved one of a prodigal who has lost his or her life, no words of mine could ever express my deepest condolences to you. There is no way I could imagine the gut-wrenching heartbreak you have endured. No one can ever explain why God would allow such a tragedy to happen, and no one on earth can ever comfort the depth of your grief. I could never fathom having to bury my children, and yet you have had to live through the injustice of outliving your child. My prayer is that God comforts you in a way that only He can and that you lean into God's power to keep living until you meet your sweet child on the other side in heaven.

For the weary parent, I know change is coming—but do not shoot off the fireworks or start the party quite yet. Sometimes during the journey of our prodigals there will be backsliding and failure. But there is a hope. You can take the word of one who has seen God deliver her own prodigals. I can assure you that your victory is on its way. God took all the artillery of the enemy (porn, alcohol, drugs, women, sex, depression and more) and made Satan wish that he had never touched my three children. Yes, the journey was long, and, at times, I wondered if I would see them make it to the age of 25. No matter how many times our children fail, fall, relapse or backslide, I pray that there is a newfound hope waiting on your horizon that tells you once again that the devil will not win.

Remember that in the heat of the battle, when it looks as if all is lost, one touch from God can change everything. There is hope for you as your heart cries out to God. He will deliver your prodigals from the spiritual war of evil as you execute the parent's battle plan and as you activate the warfare strategies. One day when your prodigal comes home, we will celebrate the victory together!

Whoever dwells in the shelter of the Most High will rest in the shadow of the Almighty. I will say of the Lord, "He is my refuge and my fortress, my God, in whom I trust." Surely he will save you from the fowler's snare and from the deadly pestilence. He will cover you with his feathers, and under his wings you will find refuge; his faithfulness will be your shield and rampart. You will not fear the terror of night, nor the arrow that flies by day, nor the pestilence that stalks in the darkness, nor the plague that destroys at midday. A thousand may fall at your side, ten thousand at your right hand, but it will not come near you. You will only observe with your eyes and see the punishment of the wicked. If you say, "The LORD is my refuge," and you make the Most High your dwelling, no harm will overtake you, no disaster will come near your tent. For he will command his angels concerning you to guard you in all your ways; they will lift you up in their hands, so that you will not strike your foot against a stone. You will tread on the lion and the cobra; you will trample the great lion and the serpent. "Because he loves me," says the LORD, "I will rescue him; I will protect him, for he acknowledges my name. He will call on me, and I will answer him; I will be with him in trouble, I will deliver him and honor him. With long life I will satisfy him and show him my salvation."

Psalm 91

Notes

Chapter 3 A Look at the Dark Army

1. "Archangel," *Merriam-Webster.com*, 2022, https://www.merriam-webster.com/dictionary/archangel.

Chapter 4 A Warrior Parent

1. "Salvation," *OxfordLearnersDictionary.com*, 2022, https://www.oxfordlearnersdictionaries.com/us/definition/english/salvation.
2. "Salvation, in Christianity," *OxfordLearnersDictionary.com*, 2022, https://www.oxfordlearnersdictionaries.com/us/definition/english/salvation.
3. "CDC: More than 1 in 3 Americans are Sleep-Deprived," *Sleep Education.org*, 2022, https://sleepeducation.org/cdc-americans-sleep-deprived/.

Chapter 8 A Different Kind of Trust

1. "Trust," *Merriam-Webster.com*, 2022, https://www.merriam-webster.com/dictionary/trust.
2. "Reliable," *Lexico.com*, 2022, https://www.lexico.com/en/definition/reliable.

Chapter 9 The Significance of Surrender

1. "Surrender," *Merriam-Webster.com*, 2022, https://www.merriam-webster.com/dictionary/surrender.

Chapter 10 Initial Responses

1. Indiana CACs, "When Yelling at a Child Becomes Verbal Abuse," *Incacs.org*, August 30, 2019, https://incacs.org/when-yelling-at-a-child -becomes-verbal-abuse/.

2. Sherry Gordon, "What Is Verbal Abuse?" *VeryWellMind.com*, February 13, 2022, https://www.verywellmind.com/how-to-recognize-verbal -abuse-bullying-4154087.

Chapter 12 Evicting Enablement

1. "Enable," *Merriam-Webster.com*, 2022, https://www.merriam-web ster.com/dictionary/enable.

2. You can find more information about this organization at https:// al-anon.org.

3. More information about Celebrate Recovery can be found at https:// www.celebraterecovery.com.

4. Meghan Rabbitt and Kaitlyn Pirie, "12 Biggest Benefits of Walking to Improve Your Health, According to Experts," *Prevention.com*, December 1, 2021, https://www.prevention.com/fitness/a20485587/benefits -from-walking-every-day/.

Chapter 13 The Voices in Our Heads

1. Elizabeth Scott, PhD, "How to Reframe Situations So They Create Less Stress," *VeryWellMind.com*, September 28, 2020, https://www .verywellmind.com/cognitive-reframing-for-stress-management-3144872.

2. Unknown source, traditionally attributed to Mark Twain.

Chapter 14 The Comfort of Community

1. "Social Isolation, Loneliness in Older People Pose Health Risks," *Nia. Nih.gov*, April 23, 2019, https://www.nia.nih.gov/news/social-isolation-lone liness-older-people-pose-health-risks#:~:text=Research%20has%20linked %20social%20isolation,Alzheimer's%20disease%2C%20and%20even%20 death.

Chapter 15 Sleuthing

1. Kirsten Weir, "Parents Shouldn't Spy on Their Kids," *Nautil.us*, April 7, 2016, https://nautil.us/parents-shouldnt-spy-on-their-kids-4524/.

2. Ibid.

Chapter 16 Handling Outside Information

1. Harper Lee, *To Kill a Mockingbird* (New York: Warner Books, 1960), 30.

Chapter 17 When the Worst Happens

1. "Rick Warren: My Son's Suicide and God's Garden of Grace," *Premier Christianity.com*, September 8, 2016, https://www.premierchristian ity.com/home/rick-warren-my-sons-suicide-and-gods-garden-of-grace /3736.article.

2. Ibid.

Chapter 18 When the Change Comes

1. Recovery Research Institute, "How Many Tries Does It Take to Resolve a Substance Use Problem? Lessons from a National Study of Recovering Adults in the U.S.," *RecoveryAnswers.org*, 2022, https://www .recoveryanswers.org/research-post/recovery-attempts-review/.

2. "Use the S.O.B.E.R Technique to Protect Your Sobriety this Christ-mas," *UK-Rehab.com*, November 27, 2014, https://www.uk-rehab.com /treatment-rehab/alcohol/use-the-sober-technique-to-protect-your-sobri ety-this-christmas/.

Laine Lawson Craft lives in Brewton, Alabama. She is a mom and a wife, and she partners with God to make impossible things become possible. She loves to accomplish this not only in her own life, but in the lives of thousands of others. She has a unique perspective because she lived through a dead marriage that was resurrected, she experienced financial breakthrough after coming close to bankruptcy, she watched her daughter be healed of a life-threatening illness, and she walked through being able to see three prodigal children be delivered and made whole, healed and free.

Many people come to Laine to receive healing from the hurts they have experienced. By guiding and encouraging many through her podcasts, online events, speaking engagements and books, Laine helps people learn that they are not alone and that it is possible to live a life they love. Many of Laine's colleagues acknowledge her as hilariously funny, energetic with a contagious laugh, approachable and real. It is through her pain and her courage to transparently share how she found victory that she helps others find healing, too. Laine has been seen on the *700 Club*, *Daystar Television*, Christian Television Network, FOX News, *Life Today TV*, Cornerstone Television, the *Christian Post* and more.

What ignites her passion about this book is having the ability to share the victory she found so that another family will not have to suffer the awful consequences of spiritual war over their prodigal child. What sets her apart from others is that this was her personal battle. All three of her teens to young adults were in war with the devil but made it through victoriously.

Over the years, her expertise has been honored and noted with accolades, including the CAN Awards, being a Selah Award Finalist and the Gold Illumination Award. She has a bestselling book, *Enjoy Today, Own Tomorrow: Discover the Power to Live the Life You Love*, and she published a nationally circulated magazine. She is a television host, a podcast host and a speaker who inspires audiences of every size, building hope and victory.

Laine also loves cooking and entertaining, walking on the beach, Pilates, singing and learning more about God. She is determined to show up as the best version of herself so that she can reach the millions of parents who are battling hell as their teens and young adults make self-destructive choices. Stories of victory are what keep her focused on her goals.

For more information on Laine or to find out how you can host a virtual Parent's Battle Plan Family Event, visit laine lawsoncraft.com.